Everyday Leadership provides an accessible, no-nonsense take on a perennial subject from the perspective that it's not just about business. This highly readable book reflects the synergy between a clinician/business advisor – Dr. Ahron Friedberg – and a lawyer/nonprofit director, Sandra Sherman. Its approach is unique: "leadership is never lonely," i.e., we lead by working (intelligently, empathetically) with others. Dr. Friedberg's up-close-and-personal guidance takes us through an array of everyday scenarios (how a trucker built a team, how an art-dealer groomed her successor) that show real people tackling real problems. Though I have been a lab head for 50 years, I still learned a lot.

Donald Pfaff, *Neurobiology and Behavior, Rockefeller University.*
Author, *How the Vertebrate Brain Regulates Behavior*

In *Everyday Leadership*, Dr. Ahron Friedberg examines the challenges of leadership from the ground up – where most people find themselves – rather than from the top-down position of the few, high, and mighty. This is a book that people can relate to, that they can use and grow with. It offers true-to-life scenarios, as Dr. Friedberg works with individuals to make the most of their leadership potential. We get up close and personal with these people, and learn along with them. *Everyday Leadership* is encouraging because it demystifies the way we can all take charge when we are called to do so.

Kerry Sulkowicz, M.D, *founder and managing principal, Boswell Group LLC, clinical professor of psychiatry, NYU Langone Medical Center*

I have been waiting for a book like *Everyday Leadership*. In the past, I have rarely been able to recommend something for people who, in the middle of busy lives, have had to step up and be larger than they thought they ever could be. But now, thanks to Dr. Ahron Friedberg, I know just what to recommend. No matter where someone is situated – just starting out, or on the way to being well-established – *Everyday Leadership* will provide solid, relatable advice that will help them meet the challenge of taking charge. It will help them grow into a new position and, especially, help them to leverage their professional relationships along the way. This book is filled with real people. It humanizes the journey towards leadership. It asks and answers the deep as well as practical questions that every leader (and potential leader) will eventually face.

Heather Berlin, Ph.D. *Cognitive Neuroscience Research Lab, Mount Sinai Health System, New York City*

Most leaders will tell you that leadership is a combination of instinct and skill. They may even say that instinct depends, in part, on character. All this is true. But beyond the generalities, what do these terms mean in practice? When does a leader know when to rely on instinct, and go with the flow? When must he or she learn skills needed to lead a specific group in a particular situation? It's these hard, real-world, rubber-hits-the-road kind of questions that *Everyday Leadership* tackles. The answers resist easy formulae, and they vary from person to person. But the virtue of this book is that it recognizes that no single answer is possible. Rather, we learn by seeing how other people address leadership challenges similar to those we may face. In this sense, Dr. Friedberg is uncommonly candid and effective. I learned lots of new approaches to leadership just by picking up on the principles that emerge from this book.

Jorge Mariscal, Ph.D. *lecturer at the SIPA School of Columbia University, New York City*

Everyday Leadership is a book that you will turn to again and again. If you are still formulating a vision of where you want to go, it will be indispensable ("How do I know what's right for me, how do I adjust when things don't turn out as expected?"). Once you are on your way, it will help you get there ("How do I leverage collaborations, how can I be flexible but still adhere to my goals?"). If you have arrived, it's there to assist you with everything from communication, to planning ahead, to mentoring the next generation of leaders. These are issues that all leaders – and potential leaders – face throughout their careers. Dr. Friedberg understands the challenges. He provides practical, incisive advice, and helps you apply it to your own situation. The questions preceding each case study, and the principles that he draws from each study, are right on target. I found myself thinking about them long after I finished reading. Actually, you don't really "finish" *Everyday Leadership* – you integrate it into how you think about leadership.

Daniel D. Bartfeld, J.D. *partner, Milbank LLP*

Everyday Leadership

Everyday Leadership examines how individuals in everyday, relatively small settings can succeed in leadership positions.

The book provides tools for tackling the unique psychological and external challenges that everyday leaders face, and offers principles that they can adapt to their own situations. Dr. Ahron Friedberg, who regularly advises leaders and would-be leaders, emphasizes the social aspect of leadership, and explores how those who are new to leadership – and those in established positions – can leverage their support networks and thrive in their roles. The book follows the experience of real people who have faced leadership challenges and learned from them, demonstrating how readers can learn from these examples and apply them to their own circumstances. Guided by a practical leadership roadmap, chapters examine concepts such as vision, determination, flexibility, planning, organization, and responsibility using extensive case studies, with reflective questions and key takeaways that help the reader consider how to apply these principles to their own leadership challenges.

This book is an essential read for HR professionals, executive coaches, management consultants, leadership trainers, and organizational psychologists as well as those facing leadership challenges in their profession.

Ahron Friedberg, M.D., is a clinical professor of psychiatry at Icahn School of Medicine at Mount Sinai, and served twice as past president of the American Society of Psychoanalytic Physicians. He is editor of *American Academy of Psychodynamic Psychiatry and Psychoanalysis Academy Forum*, and book editor of *Psychodynamic Psychiatry*, as well as a regular contributor to *Psychology Today*. He is the author with Sandra Sherman of *Through a Screen Darkly: Psychoanalytic Reflections During the Pandemic* (winner of the 2021 Gradiva Award).

Sandra Sherman, J.D., Ph.D., was a senior attorney in the U.S. government and a professor of English at two major universities. She is a director at Childsplay International. She is the author of four books and over 60 peer-reviewed articles on 18th-century literature and culture, and is co-author of several books on neuroscience. *Everyday Leadership* is the fifth book that Sandra has written with Dr. Friedberg.

Everyday Leadership

Taking Charge in the Real World

Ahron Friedberg, M.D.
with Sandra Sherman

Routledge
Taylor & Francis Group
NEW YORK AND LONDON

Designed cover image: © Zoonar GmbH / Alamy Stock Photo

First published 2024
by Routledge
605 Third Avenue, New York, NY 10158

and by Routledge
4 Park Square, Milton Park, Abingdon, Oxon, OX14 4RN

Routledge is an imprint of the Taylor & Francis Group, an informa business

ISBN: 9781032569093 (hbk)
ISBN: 9781032569116 (pbk)
ISBN: 9781003437635 (ebk)

DOI: 10.4324/9781003437635

Typeset in Times New Roman
by codeMantra

To Andrew Solomon
A leader for our generation

Contents

About the Book

At the Park Avenue Center in New York City, Dr. Ahron Friedberg advises clients with regard to issues involving leadership, as well as broader issues involving executive performance and wellness. These are middle- and upper-middle class people, e.g., still-to-be Masters of the Universe. The stories in this book are their stories. Because these people are typical of so many others, *Everyday Leadership* uses their experience to demonstrate "everyday" leadership principles. At the Center, Dr. Friedberg does not teach "rules," but helps people to develop skills that will help them become (and develop as better) leaders.

Everyday Leadership will guide readers towards how to apply these skills in their own situations. It recognizes that becoming a leader calls on a type of psychological readiness, which is part of stepping up and taking charge. Actually, at every step along the way, the Everyday Leader must learn how to measure and evaluate themselves, and be psychologically prepared if they find themselves falling short. It's okay to fall short. What matters is knowing how to acquire the mettle to keep going – and, ultimately, to improve. What Dr. Friedberg does at the Center, and in this book, is to help people develop the psychological wherewithal – along with the practical skills – to stay the course and keep improving.

Foreword

Before I read the manuscript of *Everyday Leadership*, I was struck by the cover image: a compass, no doubt from a prior century. I wondered, why had Dr. Friedberg chosen it? After all, no one uses compasses anymore, now that there is GPS. But then I understood. As we navigate the challenges of taking charge – in a complex world, without built-in guidance systems – we don't have the luxury of just following directions. Like the old sailors who *only* had compasses, we must be nimble, and exercise judgment as we encounter obstacles. In its heyday, the compass required that we calculate our own direction, even while it pointed north. When obstacles came up, it required that we make detours. How much? Up to us. As we learned from *Titanic*, it required that we think and pay attention. So, as I began to read *Everyday Leadership*, I realized that it was about how leaders really operate. They know where they want to go, and it's up to them to determine how to get there. In the process, even their destination may change. Leaders calibrate an array of factors. It's a balancing act. This sensitivity to leadership as a dynamic sets *Everyday Leadership* apart.

Dr. Friedberg wrote this book for everyone who may, at some point, need or want to take charge, as well as for anyone already in charge who senses the responsibility and potential of their position. Thus, it starts from the ground up, with real-life case studies of people with varying degrees of experience – including none. How do they formulate a vision of where they want to go? How do they develop the grit and determination to get there? The flexibility? The capacity to leverage collaborations? We follow these people in real time, up close and personal, and begin to understand how their education, in the "school of life," can inform our own.

There are no hard and fast "rules" in *Everyday Leadership* ("Do this, and everyone will fall in line behind you"). Rather, this book enables us to learn by example. As I read, I felt that if I had set out to learn how to lead, this is how I would want to learn. Each case study offers real-world insights from which the reader can draw lessons applicable to their own situation. In each study, the people try, sometimes fail, and slowly increase their awareness of what each of their challenges entails (and how they are going to meet them). They take deep dives. We benefit vicariously. Our own awareness increases as theirs does. Along the way, Dr. Friedberg provides principles – derived from these people's stories – that guide our thinking. He poses questions for us to reflect on as we read. In effect, the compass is in the background, pointing towards a direction from which we calculate on our own as we follow these people's journeys. So, I found myself thinking, "If that's what they did, then I can try my own version of it." I related to these people's stories, and saw my own challenges in theirs.

Because Dr. Friedberg is a psychiatrist, he is aware of people's psychological reactions to challenges. He appreciates that what may seem like a public performance can have significant personal ramifications. Thus, *Everyday Leadership* never trivializes the everyday. It never discounts the hard, individualized, sometimes traumatic issues that leaders face. Yet while these case studies are psychologically informed – we listen as people try to cope – they are designed primarily to follow the upward (albeit wobbly) trajectories of everyday people on their way to on increasing levels of responsibility. The studies are based on Dr. Friedberg's work at the Park Avenue Center in Manhattan, where he counsels clients (not "patients") on leadership, as well as on broader issues like executive performance and wellness. The clients are middle- and upper-middle class, but hardly Masters of the Universe. Without the supportive apparatus of large organizations, they apply what they learn as they learn it. They're less interested in rules (a one-size-fits-all mirage), than in what *works* as they integrate their personal and professional lives into a plausible modus operandi. Based on these people's experiences, we project how we might operate in similar situations though, of course, each of our own situations will be uniquely our own.

It's this toggling between what works for others and what can work for us that is the experience of reading *Everyday Leadership*. It's an immersive experience. We read, we reflect on Dr. Friedberg's questions, we apply the principles that emerge from the studies. I have never been so engaged with a book on leadership. At times, I felt as if I were in dialogue with it. Some principles struck me from the beginning – like the idea that leaders operate within networks that define but can also support them (provided they display the necessary cooperation). Some resonated with me, like the idea that collaboration is not just a division of authority, but a powerful way to enhance one's capabilities. I thought about how, in the past, I had missed opportunities (and I determined that I would not do so again). *Everyday Leadership* helps readers identify what they need to work on, even when no immediate challenges are present. It is thus a roadmap both foracquiring leadership skills and for continually honing them.

Dr. Friedberg examines aspects of leadership that he has found to be key, illustrating them through his clients' stories. These include:

- **Vision**, the need to define what we want to accomplish in view of the constraints of time, money, and our own competing needs.

- **Determination and flexibility**, so that once we understand a vision, or at least our approach to it, we find the will and external resources to pursue it.
- **Planning and organization**, the day-to-day particulars that delight MBAs but drive poets crazy.
- **Communication and collaboration**, because leadership was never meant to be lonely, and successful leaders connect with other people. They meet people where they are and bring them up to their level. They are skilled at listening and displaying empathy.
- **Responsibility**, where leaders step up and take ownership of disappointing situations without deflecting blame or offering excuses. They are responsible for mentoring the next generation of leaders, and for ensuring succession.

The case studies illuminate the intricacies of these broad areas, always within the realities of each client's situation. They feel real because they are real. The areas often overlap. So, for example, communication becomes a pivot point for exercising determination. Vision can include taking responsibility for how an organization continues to adapt. The categories are less important than the overarching insights that emerge, often kaleidoscopically as people see new possibilities, act on them, and sometimes double back to make necessary revisions. As we read, and build our own awareness, we find ourselves in one chapter – maybe Communication and Collaboration – saying "Hey, what about effective planning? You would have said the right thing if you had thought ahead." That's the way *Everyday Leadership* (and everyday leadership) works, so long as we put in the work.

I know from personal experience that leadership is hard but rewarding. There are no quick fixes. It takes effort, persistence, and the ability to tolerate measured risk. It takes a constantly expanding knowledge base. But we can practice these skills. That's where *Everyday Leadership* comes in. We can see how other people acquired those skills. Even more, Dr. Friedberg demonstrates the importance of character, for example, the need to empathize with those we lead, and to acknowledge our mistakes as part of moving on. That is, he demonstrates how personal qualities animate the professional. He sharpens our self-awareness.

To say that I benefited from *Everyday Leadership* would be an understatement. I learned so much, even when I skipped around rather than reading straight through. I also became immersed in these people's stories (I prefer that term to case studies, since I felt so involved with these people's lives). So, no matter where you are in your leadership journey, this book is necessary reading – and great reading. It's literate and intelligent. If you keep it on your nightstand, it won't lull you to sleep. You'll keep turning the pages. In every dimension that matters, it will make an impact.

Michael Warszawski
Founder and CEO of Confidence Wealth Management Partners

Acknowledgments

Someone once told me that he writes a book to learn about the subject. While this book has broader aspirations (I think leadership is a teachable skill), his approach seemed a good way to start. After all, any sort of writing allows you to articulate what you know but what may remain inchoate. In writing *Everyday Leadership*, I went back through what I'd learned by helping other people to lead, and set it out so that it would be clear, accessible, and useful to a broad array of readers.

At the Park Avenue Center in Manhattan, I have worked with many leaders – and their would-be counterparts. Over the years, this gave me the opportunity to define the leadership principles discussed in this book:

- Pursing a vision
- Exercising determination while retaining flexibility
- The need for planning and organization
- Communication and collaboration, and
- Taking responsibility

You'll read the stories of the people on whom I based these principles. These are "everyday" people who stepped up and took charge, sometimes at great personal cost. I portray their courage; their capacity to change perspective and adapt; their willingness to own their mistakes; and their will to recover and move on.

As I worked with these people, I reflected on my own career in terms of the principles that I define here. Recently, I have come into my own, fulfilling my vision to be a leader in my field of psychodynamic psychiatry. I've written books, given plenaries and presentations, become editor of a journal, and now serve as president of a national psychiatric organization. In effect, I put into practice the skill-set on which this book elaborates.

All this was hard work.

But that's the point of *Everyday Leadership*. Each of us can lead in some capacity. It doesn't have to come naturally – rather, it happens because we develop the necessary skills and diligently applied them.

Beyond what I've learned through the Park Avenue Center, I want to thank the professionals who helped shape my approach to leadership by serving as my mentors and guides. Kenneth Davis, M.D., Dennis Charney, M.D., and Rene Kahn, M.D., Ph.D., are exceptional leaders at Mount Sinai Medical Center, where I am Clinical Professor of Psychiatry. They helped me develop (and follow through on) my vision of becoming a leader in mental health and healing.

I also want to acknowledge Sandra Sherman, J.D., Ph.D. *Everyday Leadership* is our fifth book. Her clarity of mind, business acumen, and knowledge of human behavior are evident on every page. I learned so much from our conversations, and from her rigorous approach to making a point. I could not have written this book without her.

Moving forward, I hope to apply these lessons, not just to individuals but in small groups, since I've learned that we learn so much from each other. In this sense, leadership is a humbling experience. We are always learning.

Introduction

In "Traveler, your footprints," the poet Antonio Machado writes that there is no road – as we walk, we make the road. As we give ourselves to the pursuit, we pursue our own road-making.

So, who needs leaders?

More to the point, who needs another book about leadership? There are dozens already – from *The 21 Irrefutable Laws of Leadership: Follow Them and People will Follow You* (that's reassuring) to *Leadership for Dummies* (just in case you missed something). There are books based on history – *Leadership: Six Studies in World Strategy* – and those that promote a brighter future: *Inclusive Leadership: The Definitive Guide to Developing and Executing and Impactful Diversity and Inclusion Strategy*. Yet such books (instructive in their way) fail to address challenges that emerge when ordinary people must step up and take charge. These are highly personal challenges, and require personalized, unaccustomed responses. They may require adjustments in how we assess our abilities. They may even demand that we jettison norms that define our personae. Such situations, ranging from wrenching to exhilarating, are common across all organizations and social strata. They are part of living amidst complexity (aka the real world), even if our own lives are relatively simple. In this book, I address these situations.

I chose the title, *Everyday Leadership: Taking Charge in the Real World*, because "everyday" leaders take charge beyond the glare that surrounds their more prominent counterparts (e.g., crypto moguls, tech billionaires). The arenas these leaders inhabit may be no larger than a family or downtown music venue. No matter. The problems they face are just as perplexing: what compromises should I make? How can I encourage people to join my team?

But despite their commensurate challenges, everyday leaders have fewer resources – they must do more with less. They must imagine new ways to finance their projects, for example, since they may lack the credit history to reassure banks. They may need to create a persona inconsistent with who they think they really are. Is it possible to sustain the energy – the focus – for all this? Everyday leaders have no choice.

DOI: 10.4324/9781003437635-1

So, this book is about traveling through unknown territory, while making the best of the accommodations. It demonstrates that while many of the resources we call on may be internal, other people can provide essential support. Perhaps the leading, most highly-distilled idea in *Everyday Leadership* is that leadership is collaborative: It need not be lonely at the top. Many people are potentially a source of support. We need to learn how to tap it, assess it, and apply it without unduly compromising our work.

"Compromise" comes up again and again in *Everyday Leadership*, since it denotes both cooperation with others – necessary if we are to survive – and dilution, since too much can undermine what we set out to do. So, making the best of things entails a balancing act, where we draw on other people's help without giving away the store as a *quid pro quo*. It's a skill that everyday leaders employ every day.

In view of its unique challenges, everyday leadership is not just a subcategory of Leadership (just as children are not simply little adults). It's similar – to a degree – but on a smaller scale. I first hit on the concept through my work at the Park Avenue Center in Manhattan, where an array of my clients' issues coalesced into what I would later define as "everyday leadership." Many of these issues involved relationships that, while not primarily emotional, had a higher emotional/psychological content than we conventionally associate with managerial challenges. I was sensitive to these issues because, while the Center is a non-medical consultancy, I am a psychiatrist. My work at the Center, which is distinct from my psychiatric practice, is necessarily psychologically informed. Thus, my approach to everyday leadership is so informed, at the Center and now in this book. I draw on my clinical experience and psychological training, as well as on current psychosocial research.

At the Center, I consult with clients (not "patients") who need help with issues involving leadership, as well as broader issues involving executive performance and wellness. These are middle- and upper-middle class people, e.g., still-to-be Masters of the Universe. They are relatable. The stories in this book – their stories – are short case studies preceded by additional commentary, based on consultations that I've had over the years. Because these people are typical of so many others, *Everyday Leadership* uses their experience as the basis for teaching certain basic "everyday" leadership principles. At the Center, I do not teach "rules," but show people how to develop certain skills that will help them lead.

Nonetheless, *Everday Leadership* will guide readers towards how to apply these skills in their own situations. It recognizes that becoming a leader calls on a type of psychological readiness, which is part of stepping up and taking charge. Actually, at every step along the way, the Everyday Leader must learn how to measure and evaluate themselves, and be psychologically prepared to find themselves falling short. It's okay to fall short. What matters is knowing how to acquire the mettle to keep going – and, ultimately, to improve. Part of what I do at the Center, and do in this book, is help people develop the psychological wherewithal to stay the course and keep improving.

Leaders need to believe in themselves. They are never effective if they are grudging or half-hearted. Anyone can pick up on a reluctant leader, and they will find someone else. So, part of being psychologically ready to lead is being convinved that the task is worthwhile. As a general matter, it *is* worthwhile. Leaders are change agents. They alter the course of history. By their example, they give people confidence to go out and perform themselves. They provide direction and energy – like Roger Bannister, who broke the four-minute mile in 1954. After that, people knew the so-called barrier *could* be broken, and then it was, again and again. What was extraordinary became, in effect, everyday. Bannister was inspiring. The movie about him – *Chariots of Fire* (1981) – is contagiously inspiring.

Of course, it is possible to multiply examples endlessly. How about Gandhi, who helped found a nation, or Henry Ford? Even Jeff Bezos, though you might not like his methods. Leadership is important. Think of the world before and after these people, and you get the point. Though Everyday Leaders operate on a smaller scale, their work is a version of the leaders we all know. In *Everyday Leadership*, I focus on how to fully invest in your own leadership potential, and then pursue it effectivly. How do you energize people, and impart your energy to them? How do you help them see that the road ahead, as you envision it, is worth the trek? Leadership, even in relatively scaled-down contexts, is a combination of the practical and the visionary.

If leadership were not this complex mix of present tense and (ideally) future perfect – i.e., if it weren't so central to how people organize their lives – we wouldn't recognize and celebrate it as we do. Our culture features holidays named after leaders. Take, for example, Martin Luther King Day or Presidents Day . . . or Christmas, named after the founder of Christianity. We take time every year to think about how these people altered our collective experience. It makes us feel good that these people existed. This is no fluke. Neuronal research has shown that leadership is a fact of human organizational strategy. In "Understanding social hierarchies: The neural and psychological foundations of status perception," Jessica Koski et al. (2015) observe that "We undoubtedly vary in the skills and traits we possess, and when choosing the appropriate person to listen to, follow, or emulate, we want someone with the skills and traits we consider the most desirable or important." It is possible to identify this principle throughout history and even in lab experiments with animals. The point is that leadership is woven into social organization and, in most cases, we are glad that it is.

Because the leadership issues that each of us face are so personal, so bound up with particularizing, local situations, *Everyday Leadership* does not lay down "infallible" rules (either for becoming a leader or for managing in that position). That would miss the subtlety and spontaneity of how each of us may be required to respond. It would miss the jerry-built nature of leadership on a small scale, where we accomplish what we can and then think up new, possibly more productive strategies that utilize the resources at hand. So, this book suggests broad, individually adaptable principles for coping with challenges as they arise – that is, as we evolve into a leadership role and adapt as we go. (Note the term "role," since it is often true that our public, leadership persona is out of sync with how we perceive ourselves.)

From this perspective, everyday leadership is situational, a way of managing challenges so that they do not prevent us from reaching a goal that has not been unduly compromised. Does this sound modest? Welcome to the real world (and why I chose the book's subtitle). Apart from conforming to some basic principles ("I will always treat my colleagues fairly," "I will always be honest"), we may be required to change course too often for one overarching approach to govern how we proceed.

I've been down this unmarked road before. When I wrote *Towards Happiness: A Psychoanalytic Approach to Finding Your Way* (2022), I argued that no one can tell anyone how to be happy. That is, each of us finds our own way, based on the circumstances of our lives. A similar principle applies to everyday leadership, since it's futile to lay down managerial rules for the unique challenges that everyday leaders face. What does help, however – and as I argued in *Happiness* – is that we can learn from how others, in similar circumstances, navigated their own challenges. The stories in this book are intended for that purpose, i.e., to illustrate how ordinary people (at least in terms of their status) managed to step up and lead. Their approaches can be adapted as need be, recognizing that every approach to leadership must change in response to the demands of their situation.

However, even though I just issued a disclaimer (albeit one that is true to life), I think certain general, adaptable principles can inform our understanding of effective leadership. I want to highlight these principles here. Perhaps the most important is that leaders are in constant negotiation with the led (and with those whom they seek to lead). A leader cannot be effective absent loyalty from the people they lead, and – to earn it and keep it – they must reassure such people that there are benefits from the relationship, and that the project is worthwhile. This may require compromise, so that everyone tangibly experiences the benefit. Viewed in this light, leadership is an exercise in building relationships. It is presumptuous for a leader to think "Well, I'll go it alone, and have it all my way." Most challenges are too big (even on the reduced scale of everyday leadership) for one person to manage single-handedly. They will need a team, and teams need to feel that they have the leader's support. So, even as circumstances evolve, no leader can stand apart, either from the troops or from the network of people on whom they rely for advice, expertise, and material support.

Another principle I want to cite is the need for empathy. A leader must never forget that they lead real people, with their own needs, interests (and, yes, challenges). It is crucial – if one is to gain and keep such people's trust – to respond to their concerns. Strategically, a leader must *understand* such concerns so they can respond in ways that allow people to feel like more than just cogs in a machine. Again, compromise may be necessary. But people will likely require less if they feel that you care about them, that you take them into account as you move ahead.

Compromise is the result of flexibility. So, while leaders should be determined, they should never be rigid. They should listen and weigh options. Sometimes they must listen to themselves, as they debate internally their various possible courses of action. In *Everyday Leadership*, I pair flexibility with determination in one chapter, since plowing ahead with a leadership initiative can fail without accepting some likely redirection. In the un-lonely world of the leader, flexibility may become the defining M.O. It is the foundation of communication and collaboration. It should be embedded in planning (the subject of another chapter), both near- and long-term.

In my discussion so far, character traits have segued into ways of responding to practical challenges. This is because they are hardly separable. An everyday leader must empathize to appreciate constituents' needs and compromise accordingly. They should be flexible in order to work with teams they rely on. A leader develops useful character traits so that their actions do not seem forced – a matter of expedience rather than genuine concern. While some people in this book "play a good game" (it's all they're capable of), most literally work on themselves, learning to think like a leader as if that were their natural inclination.

In this vein, another principle I want to cite is that leaders always learn as they go, never discarding useful insights – even where these result from failure. They become more sensitive, literally more conscious of themselves as leaders. Thus, in one story, I show how determination results from positive feedback, where an emerging self-awareness creates – and benefits from – the ability to seize opportunities as they emerge; those opportunities lead to enhanced self-awareness. Being a leader is never static, even with your title on the door. Learning how to lead (in context with the demands of one's own situation) is part of leading. Picking up the pieces and starting over is never a waste of time, but just an aspect of learning. We can learn as much from failure as from success, sometimes more.

Of course, I could cite other leadership principles, like the need for self-discipline and a willingness to acknowledge responsibility (even when things don't turn out well). I could mention that leaders must know how to communicate and collaborate. But these skills are straight-forward, and I wanted to highlight here (i.e., right up front) those that are more nuanced. I devote whole chapters of this book to straight-forward (and very important) capabilities, but traits like empathy and the ability to make strategic compromises run through every chapter. They are foundational to an everyday leader's success.

So, my larger point is that leaders do not merely bring to the task the skills that they have. They enhance these skills, and develop new ones. The process – and it is a process – calls for a high degree of continued self-awareness, an ability to take stock of oneself in a situation as the situation changes. You should look at yourself honestly, and register people's responses. You should take account of those responses. When a client asks me "How do I become a leader?" I say that you have to live in a world of two-way mirrors. You look out at people looking in, and when you see how they react you either keep-on-keeping-on or change accodingly. Leaderrship is a dynamic process, where leading and *becoming* a leader are inseparable.

I should also note that principles that are inner-facing, and apply to a leader and his or her employees, are also outer-facing, and apply to how a leader engages with clients (or potential clients). A leader knows how to keep clients interested and committed.

Everyday Leadership examines certain aspects of leadership that I have found to be key, illustrating them through my clients' stories. The first chapter, "Vision," concerns the need for leaders (and their would-be counterparts) to define what they want to accomplish in view of the constraints of time, money, and their own competing needs. Do you want to build a specialty transportation company, run a family business, strike out on your own in real estate? Well, there may be compromises you'll need to make, and a lot of false starts that you'll have to double back on. So, what degree of compromise and disappointment can you accept? How do you maintain your initiative? How do you put together a support network, and recalibrate your vision as you experience its implications in your own life and the lives of people around you? How do you muster the internal and external resources you need? My clients' stories demonstrate how they dealt with similar challenges.

The second chapter, "Determination and Flexibility" examines how – once you understand your vision, or at least your approach to it – you find the will and external resources to pursue it. Throughout, *Everyday Leadership* approaches emotional/psychological and mundane practical considerations of leadership together, since that is how they occur in the world. Accordingly, this chapter examines how flexibility (and its necessary component, empathy) are part of a determined pursuit of a guiding vision. It examines how to be flexible while still maintaining your advantage. It examines the need to develop trust among people in the widening penumbra of those affected by your initiatives. In this sense, it is about maintaining balance among the various competing considerations that you will encounter along the way, always recognizing that "balance" is not the same as stasis – the strategies that you use to remain determined are always likely to change.

The third chapter, "Planning and Organization," is largely about logistics. In this sense, it is a counterpart to Chapter Two, extending it into day-to-day particulars that delight MBAs but drive the poets crazy. If we like to think grand thoughts, how do we develop an interest in the nitty-gritty? How (conversely) do we conceptualize the big picture? Can we know what's coming next, and when to emphasize what? Planning and organization are as much a source of anxiety as pursuing a vision and are, in fact, just down-to-earth versions of that pursuit. Moreover, as in every stage of everyday leadership, we'll have to deal with issues of compromise. How can we rely on others to take the organizational reins without surrendering our initial vision? This becomes a particular challenge as our enterprise grows and matures. My clients have faced all these issues.

In a way, the fourth chapter, "Communication and Collaboration," embodies the essence of *Everyday Leadership*, in that it is based on the idea that leadership is never lonely. An everyday leader – who seeks help where they can find it – must connect with other people. They need to make themselves understood and, ideally, appreciated. To move their plans forward, they need to inspire. Such connection is ongoing, even though whom they connect with and how they connect may change. The point is that leaders are networkers, moving like nodes in a kaleidoscope. I have used the term "connection" here because it is general – it applies to both communication and collaboration. But if you think about it, effective communication is a prerequisite of collaboration. They're joined at the hip, like determination and flexibility. Thus, collaboration is impossible unless the leader makes their case. The stories in this chapter illustrate ways of effectively communicating which, as I have already suggested, requires a type of empathy that we might not otherwise extend to those who are not our intimates or even well-known to us.

The fifth chapter, "Responsibility," concerns a character trait necessary to everyday leaders who must step up and take ownership of disappointing situations without deflecting blame or offering excuses. Assuming responsibility tests a leader's mettle, and can determine what people think of them over the long haul. Is this leader honest? Is he or she strong, and strategic enough to get out in front of situations before the fallout overtakes a whole enterprise? These are major questions, if only because trust is so crucial to a leader's continuing success. However, responsibility also refers to looking after a project or an enterprise so that its wheels stay well-oiled and everyone involved with it stays employed, satisfied, and high-functioning. It requires clearing away obstacles, as well as mentoring the next generation of leaders and vital employees. So, responsibility is almost about cultivating what might be considered old-fashioned virtues, in the face of more prominent leaders who think of themselves as hired problem-solvers and never commit themselves long-term. Responsibility, therefore, comes back around to having and pursuing a vision in the right way. In the long-term, a vision falters unless the one pursuing it displays responsibility.

As may seem obvious by now, the topics of these chapters intersect. You can't, for example, devise a good plan unless you're flexible. So, the implication is that everyday leaders need to be well-rounded, and develop an array of qualities needed to confront the various challenges that they will face. Of course, this takes time, and some leaders are born on third base. But as the stories in *Everyday Leaders* demonstrate, people usually find the means when the pressure is on. They survive.

It is encouraging that modern neuroscience is on the side of this book's approach to leadership as a social activity. Donald Pfaff's *Origins of Human Socialization* (2021) observes that "It is crucial to understand the compelling evidence for our natural sociable affinities. . . By 'affinity' I mean a spontaneous natural liking or sympathy for another person, an interest in forming a bond or relationship." Prof. Pfaff traces the development of hearing and sight, for example, and examines how they contributed to humans' becoming so "naturally" social. He examines the brain mechanisms involved in socialization, and our related genetics. *Everyday Leadership* is situated alongside this discourse, arguing that ordinary people have the natural capacity to assume leadership roles. We should work with this capacity. We should work *on* it if we've never ventured outside our comfort zones. But that's not to say that we can't if we want to.

Based on everything I've learned, *Everyday Leadership* will seek to delineate the principles emerging from the case studies that it offers. It also raises specific questions so that readers can envision – can actually formulate – how these principles apply to their own situations. It provides sufficient structure so that readers feel confident in extrapolating, that is, in thinking creatively about their own leadership challenges. The book offers a strong helping hand, even as it does not condescend, or pretend that everyone's challenges will be amenable to predetermined advice. *Everyday Leadership* recognizes that leadership, as a process, is defined by learning and continual adjustment.

Of course, if you embark on a leadership project, no matter how challenging, it's still only part of your life. You are still You. That is, you need to know when to wind down, stop obsessing, and live a life outside of taking charge. Thus, even if you are laser-focused on the job, you can kick back when you're back home. Leaders should remember how to relax. They should learn to separate themselves from work.

By the same token, they should not let purely personal aspirations infiltrate their work. You might think, "Oh, I want to be liked." But catch yourself, and recognize that that's your everyday-self talking – not your Everyday Leader talking. You should maintain a discrete distance between the two, adjusted as appropriate to the situation. If you are leading a business, your personal demeanor should not be determined by how you'd like to be regarded by your friends. If you are heading some family project, you still need to maintain your authority, and accommodate family dynamics only insofar as they do not overwrite your objectives. In time, you should learn that Who you are and What you are will not always be the same.

This last idea is important. Some of the world's best leaders have been model managers, and less than admirable in their personal lives. That's unenviable but, at least, these people kept their personal proclivities personal, and did not allow them to affect their job performance. They knew how to remain professionally disciplined, even if their after-hours lives were fodder for the tabloids. Most likely, Everyday Leaders will never be under the public microscope but, in principle, the need to separate their personal and workplace demeanors is the same.

Finally, I should note that while this is not a medical text, I have tried to be considerate of and protect my clients' confidentiality as much as possible. I have generally followed principles employed by similarly situated authors in handling case material. The dialogues reflect my conversations in consultation but, again, they have been scrubbed to ensure my clients' privacy.

References

Friedberg, Ahron with Sandra Sherman. *Towards Happiness: A Psychoanalytic Approach to Finding Your Way* (New York: Routledge), 2022.

Kissinger, Henry. *Leadership: Six Studies in World Strategy* (New York: Penguin), 2022.

Koski, Jennifer et al. "Understanding social hierarchies: The neural and psychological foundations of status perception," *Social Neuroscience* 10:5, 527–50 (2015).

Loeb, Marshall and Stephen Kindel. *Leadership for Dummies* (New York: Wiley), 1999.

Machado, Antonio. "Traveler, your footprints," https://www.poetryfoundation.org/poems/58815/traveler-your-footprints.

Maxwell, John. *The 21 Irrefutable Laws of Leadership: Follow Them and People Will Follow You* (New York: Harper Collins), 2022.

Pfaff, Donald. *Origins of Human Socialization* (Cambridge: Academic Press), 2021.

Sweeney, Charlotte and Fleur Bothwick. *Inclusive Leadership: The Definitive Guide to Developing and Executing and Impactful Diversity and Inclusion Strategy* (Harlow, U.K.: Pearson), 2016.

Chapter 1

Vision

In the Introduction, I defined vision as the objective that leaders ultimately work towards. "Ultimately" is crucial because you may not, early in your development, be committed to a particular vision or even know that it exists. Over time, however, it becomes clear. The stories in this chapter describe that process. How do you discover a vision and, finally, marshal the will to achieve it? How do you sort through competing visions? Ultimately, so to speak, what's required is personal maturation – which can occur, as I demonstrate, at any age.

But there's more. While psychological factors play a huge part in achieving your vision, there are practical considerations as well. It's one thing to know that you have a vision, and even to know that you'll do what it takes to achieve it. It's quite another to break down "what it takes" into nuts and bolts – the actual, practical steps that enable leaders to get on with leading. This chapter examines the nuts and bolts along with the psychology. Thus, in addition to demonstrating how leaders came to understand their vision, it considers what they did to pursue it. We look at both sides of the coin.

This chapter will make several points – for example, that a vision can change shape, and that *we* change as we seek to achieve it. But one point worth emphasizing, right up front, is the need to let go of proprietary notions regarding one's "own" personal vision. As the following stories show, a vision is always inflected by other people's ideas. Even by other people's visions. Without others' expertise and support, we might be unable to formulate an achievable vision. Without teamwork and networking, a vision might remain a tiny, local phenomenon – no bigger than one's head. Without a willingness to compromise, we might be dismissed as pig-headed. So, we must recognize that a vision (however idealistic) cannot be idealized. It is always up for revision or, rather, negotiation. It is formed in a process of letting-go or, more propitiously, of give-and-take.

Thus, no leader is an island. He or she must take account of a vision's stakeholders – including those people being led. But if that makes a vision vulnerable in some sense, it is also a benefit. By remaining receptive to others, our learning curve is perpetually on the upswing. As the stories in his chapter show, the most successful leaders are always learning.

DOI: 10.4324/9781003437635-2

Finally, I would like to observe that Everyday Leaders are not just big-time leaders writ small – while their sphere is scaled down, their modus operandi differs in *kind*. They have no built-in, always on-call networks of consultants, image-makers, and pollsters to help them shape (let alone achieve) their vision. In the political sphere, for example, or among the Masters of the Universe, we often hear about unnamed but influential (and highly-paid) "advisors." In fact, most Masters have networks that support them without even being asked, just because they want to stay on retainer. Accordingly, these leaders experience less conflict about their visions (which has been vetted and focus-grouped in advance by professionals, who keep on honing it as conditions change). They walk out into the world self-assured. But for everyday leaders, achieving a vision requires strenuous efforts on an intimate scale, both in defining their vision and achieving it. It requires a degree of flexibility, spontaneity, and quick reaction that big-time leaders rarely require. They must keep looking around them, 360°.

It's not easy. But it's possible.

Having a workable vision is the first, indispensable step to becoming an everyday leader. Through a certain amount of trial and error, you can learn how to manage your vision. Then you're on your way. So, as you read these stories, pay attention to the *process* of how each person finds, acknowledges, and then adjusts their vision to maintain it. These are key steps. No one just "has" a vision. Like everything in life, a vision is dynamic. As it changes, we grow into it. Observe how the people in these stories *pay attention* to their vision – they do not allow it to get beyond their capabilities or, in another key, drive every aspect of their lives to the exclusion of everything else. A vision must be situated, that is, integrated into your life so that your life remains workable, even satisfying. It can't be allowed to take over your life like kudzu. Attending to your vision is, itself, a skill.

***

It's rare that a vision springs fully formed from our imagination. Experience down the road will help to define it. Other people will help to sustain it. In this sense, vision has an element of good fortune or chance. Maybe even luck. But, of course, we can make the most of these. If chance breaks our way, we should think about how to take the best advantage of it. When we meet someone who can help us, we can't be shy – actually, we should be as forthcoming as possible, enlisting them on our behalf, prevailing on their good will. We can't invest so much personal capital in a vision that it becomes rigid, an extension of ourselves and our egos. We should, instead, accept that a vision is always porous, and that other influences can shape it over time.

The following story concerns the synergy of good luck and meeting the right people. But, more fundamentally, it's about how one lucky guy made the most of his opportunities. He wanted to become a physician/writer, and met an editor who challenged him to think about how to create a new genre of medical writing. He took up the challenge and worked at it, ultimately recruiting more people to help support his work. He parlayed writing into intellectual leadership.

What we learn, is that if leadership starts with a vision, we must look behind that vision to how that leader came to understand and develop it. Often the process hinges on the unexpected. Leadership requires the ability to seize the unexpected, and turn it to advantage. It requires accepting that a vision may look different from one day to the next, until finally it settles into what it should be. "Should" means what works best for us, given all the complex circumstances that we must navigate.

Notice how, in this story, my client easily moves on from emulating his heroes – world-famous physician/writers – to take up leadership of a kind of writing that he could do. His ego never gets in the way. Rather, he allows it to motivate him towards a practicable goal. This demonstrates maturity. Satisfying his ego meant altering his initial vision for something more sustainable. But because his vision finally seemed anchored in his own demonstrable experience, he found people willing to sustain it.

So, as you read this story, think of acquiring your own, personal vision as a process of letting go. That is, it may be impractical to take on inspiration – probably from some hero – without also refracting it through your own. What comes out may be diminished in one sense but, in another, it may be well-adapted to where you can go. Ask yourself:

- *In formulating a vision, how much of what I admire in someone else's career is practical in my own? Am I being honest, and not letting pride guide my aspirations?*
- *How much of my original vision am I willing to forego, even as I still pursue it?*
- *How can I make the most of encounters with ther people to shape my vision? Do I know how to interest people in my ideas, and how to elicit their most helpful responses?*
- *Am I willing to change my vision as my career develops? That is, do I understand that it must evolve along with my evolving circumstances?*

If you answered No to any of these questions, then you know where to focus your efforts. Part of maintaing a practical vision is to let it go with the flow of your life. "Flow" in this regard is non-linear, and includes productive interactions with other people. They see you from a perspective that, by definition, you do not have. Often, they have experience that you wish you had. So now, watch how my client deals with the type of issues I have just cited, and measure how you would have reacted. Feel free to criticize him, but also learn from how his vision matures.

Future Forward

Leaders Find People who Can Help to Refine and Sustain Their Vision

Leadership means having a vision of your future – then, sometimes, creating a cast of characters to sustain it. Consider Larry, who had just graduated pre-med from college but wanted to be a physician/writer like Chekhov, Conan Doyle, or Michael Chrichton. How, he asked, did they achieve such vast cultural power? How did they conscript battalions of intermediaries (publishers, critics, film-makers) who made their vision a practical reality?

When he came to see me, Larry was heading to London for a gap year, mainly to study biophysics but also to play in a folk-rock band with British students he'd met online. "Maybe I can write about being a part-time musician," he told me. "I need *something* to write about." It seemed plausible. So off he went, a grad student by day and a folkie after hours. We'd Skype twice a week, often while he was writing up some bio results late at night (it was five hours earlier in New York).

I had hoped that playing with the group would give him some insight into group dynamics, and that – ultimately – he'd turn what he learned into a short story.

It didn't happen.

But something more interesting did. During several bleak weekends, the group performed at a local hospital, mainly for immobilized patients. They'd wheel themselves into a recreation area where the group would set up. Larry, who had always loved the flute, got to play a few solos. He was a hit, and afterwards, when the rest of the group's had gone home, he'd stay and talk with his fans. Since he was headed to medical school, he saw the time spent away from his lab as part of the next phase of his education.

He also had an ulterior motive. He sensed that here was a topic to write about.

As Larry hung out with the patients, he realized that British hospitals felt much "homier" than their American counterparts. Even patients who couldn't get around had lots of company. In addition to the musical performances, tea was served in the rec area several times a day. There were sing-alongs and storytelling competitions. The place was made to feel like a small town, albeit with a population that hoped to walk out the door. The communality was striking. It made the time pass, and diminished the sense of isolation. Larry even heard people plan to meet up when they finally left.

Finally, he told me that while he was not, perhaps, creative like Chekhov or Chrichton, he knew he had things to say. He wanted to tell people's stories, and to compare the humane practices that he found in a British hospital to the rigidly clinical environments of their American counterparts. "I guess this is medical sociology," he said. "You know, like how the culture of a place influences the treatment of patients." Larry had seen enough BBC TV to appreciate the near fetishizing of village life in Britain. So, his argument, it seemed, was that even in London the value placed on village life infiltrated hospital settings. A fascinating idea.

Over the next several weeks, between working in his lab and performing with the band, Larry wrote an article and submitted it to a medical journal. He wrote an abstract citing "empirical research," and included comparative "data" from visits to British and American hospitals (the latter examples were thin, but he claimed they were representative). He identified himself as a graduate student who would enter medical school in the fall. He sent a resume and a transcript. He received a polite rejection.

My job is to talk people through disappointment. "Come on, Larry," I said. "This is your first outing, and you're hardly a conventional author with a university position." I suggested that he not give up. Perhaps he could talk with the editor, and find out what the article still needed. "I think it needs an M.D. or a Ph.D.," he said. "And probably they're not used to articles without a lot of numbers and technical terms." "So, expand their horizons," I said, even while I wasn't sure how I would do that.

Yet with the energy of someone convinced of his own good idea, Larry emailed the editor for an appointment, explaining that he could demonstrate the validity, novelty, and importance of his observations. He emailed twice, and then left a message. Later, he told me that he could see how what he'd written might become part of a larger project – a whole field comparing the integration of culture and hospital administration – and that the article was, perhaps, its leading edge. In his mind, anyway, Larry was founding a new research area.

He waited. We waited. Finally, the editor's assistant called to say that while the editor was still unpersuaded, he realized that Larry was a committed researcher. Since the editor was planning to attend a lecture at Larry's university, he'd be happy to meet for tea in the cafeteria later that afternoon (clearly, he'd gone out of his way to be informal). Larry accepted. He thought at least he might learn something.

When they finally did meet, Larry was prepared. "I told him about all the future articles that people could write on this topic once they realized that it *was* a topic. I suggested that social science methodologies could be deployed." In other words, Larry attempted to interest the editor in becoming a pioneer. As Larry described the conversation, I could see that the whole experience, including rejection, had bolstered his sense of himself as a ground-breaker. What started as an article had, over a few weeks, become a focus for Larry's future work as a physician/writer.

***

As it turned out, and after much back and forth, Larry and the editor came to an agreement. The article, as written, simply lacked the technical apparatus to be published *as* an article. But it was still interesting. The editor offered to publish it as a Guest Opinion, without the imprimatur of peer review. "We have those, occasionally," the editor told him, "and they provoke significant response." Larry couldn't believe his luck.

But as I told him, he shouldn't regard it as mere luck. In effect, the editor had challenged him to think harder and longer – and with more technical fire-power – about his initial perceptions. He had invited Larry to grow into his ideas and even lead a nascent field. I urged him to take up the challenge, since it could provide an entrée into becoming a physician/writer. He was a leader in the field, provided he could demonstrate that it could be a field.

Fast forward to medical school. No more moonlighting as a flautist. Yet Larry still had a little time, and spent it talking to sociology professors, who were supportive. Since he was allowed one course per year outside the medical school, he chose Social Science Methods the first year and, the second year, he audited one that applied such methods to health care. By the third year, when he had begun making rounds, he made his move. He started a journal. He raised funds from the Dean (who had a soft-spot for interdisciplinary studies), and found a couple of investors among alumni. He found editors among his friends at school, and appointed an Advisory Board of professors from the medical school and the social sciences.

So now there is a journal devoted to comparative hospital administration.

But more to the point, there is now a leader of a new field. Larry had a vision, both for himself and for an area of research that had yet to develop. By making the most of strategic connections, he turned that vision into reality. What started as his personal vision of becoming a physician/writer became, over time, a vehicle for him to express himself in that capacity. From the outset, when he had tea with that British editor, he had to bring people along with him. He succeeded then, and continued.

Larry exemplifies leaders who have a vision, both for themselves and for projects that will sustain their personal growth. I emphasize growth, since his vision evolved over time, along with his ability to achieve it.

Now that you have read Larry's story, think about:

- How disappointment can be turned to your advantage. Larry conforms his vision to what he learns is possible.
- Whether you have been dissuaded by disappointment. Do you give up easily, or are you willing to take a chance on something outside your comfort zone?
- Jump-starting your vision by getting people on board with it. One supporter leads to another.

The point is not to give up, but to envision possibilities and make the most of them – often by raising interest among people who can support you. As I noted at the outset, a personal vision is rarely just the product of one's own aspiration. It's inflected, i.e., the product of many minds – including, but not exclusively, yours. Of course, once it's in place, you can make the most of it, which Larry does.

As we just saw, no one is born a leader. Leaders evolve. They adapt to conditions and, ideally, make the most of them. They learn from setbacks and mistakes, and by looking around at everyone else's. When they experience success, they do not take it for granted. Their lives as leaders are a work in progress. As they pursue a vision of what they want to achieve, they rarely travel in a straight line. They are, rather, changing just to keep up and, even by indirection, get ahead. The best ones have certain fixed principles – like loyalty to their staff – but everything else is up for continual evaluation. Having a vision makes no practical sense if you can't make the most of your moment.

So, leadership is a constant negotiation between who and where you are, and who and what is pulling you in other directions. Usually, people want you to satisfy <u>*their*</u> *vision (sometimes even their vision of your vision). If for example, you want to market a new product, how do you project the competence to strike out on your own? It's a balancing act, somewhere between fake-it-till-you-make-it (not the best approach for the risk averse) and making an impact with dazzling research (which you may not have). If you can toggle around in the middle, and keep learning and adapting, you might arrive at a place where you're credible.*

Your objective is to learn from the competition, rather than to succumb. While adversity is always there, your objective is to find ways over, around, and through. Leadership is like some engineering project where the lines on the map are rarely straight. The point of the project is to get from A to B, however many detours and obstacles need to be cleared.

In this story, we follow one of my clients who learns how to lead by adapting to changes surrounding a company that he inherits. He could have remained complacent and, probably, earned a pretty good living. But he had a vision that propelled him to learn how to adapt to changes and turn them to his advantage. When he didn't know something, he hired people who could teach him. He built teams of experts. He discovered that No Leader is An Island. Leaders function as part of rapid-response teams that tackle adversity and beat it back.

In our own lives, we can be guided by a vision but, nonetheless, be willing to take on board people who know more than we do. We become no less a leader by acknowledging what we don't know. So, as you read, ask yourself:

- *Am I willing to learn from the competition without risking my ego? Does stiff competition scare or energize me?*
- *Is good-enough okay with me? If not, how can I take my vision to he next level? What sorts of people will have the will and expertise to support me?*
- *How can I become a successful team player, while still remaining in charge?*
- *Am I good at diagnosing problems so that I can choose the right people to tackle them? If not, how do I learn to find probelms so that they can be addressed?*

Good leaders develop an instinct for motivating others to believe in their vision – and for keeping them involved as the vision evolves. They share the credit and the perks. But while we have heard a lot about a Team of Rivals – people who work together but have disparate interests and give dffering advice – it's best to start out with people who put your interests ahead of their ulterior motives. You need to conserve energy for your project, rather than for quelling internecine battles and figuring out who's ostensibly right.

Before you choose a support team, however, you should have (or develop) a good grasp of near- and medium-term problems so that you can choose the right team(s) to support you. This usually necessitates taking a deep dive into every aspect of a project, rather than just orchestrating teams to do it for you. There is a delicate balance between second-guessing your expert teams and taking their advice without question. This requires judgment which, in turn, develops with coming to grips with every aspect of your project. You'll have to muck around and get your hands dirty (as my client does). To creat something as a leader is to build it, piece by piece, and all the pieces need to fit.

Adaptation

Effective Leadership Requires Effective Team Building (often with Multiple, Specialized Teams)

"Adaptation" might be the title of Burt's life story. Burt was a fortyish guy obsessed with intermodal transportation: freight cars with containers off-loaded onto barges, then locally onto trucks. When he turned up in my office, his vision was to become the country's largest intermodal shipper of refrigerated produce. It was not glamorous – like starting a hedge fund or launching an app – but it was grounded in the undeniable reality that food needs to get to people who will eat it.

Burt inherited his vision. His grandfather had owned a fleet of trucks, and was known in the city for on-time, reliable deliveries. His father had joined the business, but when he tried to expand into the tri-state area he was clobbered by Mob operators. The experience almost killed him (literally), and the business barely survived. Even at its best, it could not meet industry standards in technology and logistics. While some small grocers continued to use it, they did so only because they could demand below-market rates. Burt was determined to rescue the firm, to bring it into the 21st century . . . and then to become a real player.

"Okay," he told me. "I know it's a challenge. But I see the possibilities." Burt had worked in the business since college, mainly in accounts receivable, but now he succeeded his father as president. "It's up to me," he said. We talked about where to start and, more fundamentally, how to jump from back-office inconsequence (The Boss' Son) into leadership. Who would take him seriously? Could he raise capital, build an expert team going forward?

Burt's father had started grooming him to take over, and had introduced him around, but had never allowed him to get involved enough to credibly run the business – salespeople, dispatchers, drivers, contractors, facilities maintenance, truck maintenance, billing, purchasing, i.e., a world of interlocking pieces that had to be coordinated and, as Burt now saw it, massively upgraded. For example, "sales" had to become CRM (Customer Relations Management). Dispatch had to segue into logistics. The challenge was huge. But, as we talked, he thought maybe it didn't matter that nothing was quite right. "I'm going to reinvent the place," he said. "That means watching, calculating, recalibrating every day."

His idea was that you don't just "grow a business." You *allow* it to grow by tackling problems head-on – with everything you've got – so that they don't get worse. So that they don't make everything else a problem. So that they finally disappear, and let you tackle the next problem. "I take a scorched earth approach to problems," he said. "No denial, no delay, just wipe them out." Yikes. How did some guy from accounts receivable come up with that idea?

In college, Burt had been the captain and quarterback of his frat-house football team. He was a motivator. When he saw shoddy playing, he called it out. He would analyze the opposing team's moves, and devise new plays to block them. When he was on the field, he played as if his life depended on winning, and he expected a similar commitment from everyone. "I'm a team builder," he said, "and teams solve problems." He knew that running an interstate business was not exactly intramural football, but he thought that his approach was scalable. "In college, I got those guys to adapt over the season," he told me. "We began to win more games by bigger margins." What I heard was: 1) team building, and 2) teaching the team to adapt.

We discussed how all this would play out, so to speak, in building a next-gen, Not-Your-Father's shipping company. Burt hired a group of software engineers to analyze the potential tri-state market, spot bottlenecks, calculate effective price points for the various sub-markets, and produce an algorithm that would allow him to adjust going forward. "I wanted to be on top of the market," he said, "not just following the big guys. I needed a continuing source of intelligence that my salespeople could use." Those salespeople were now learning to use CRM, to stay in touch with customers and monitor their daily, seasonal, annual needs on a product-by-product basis. You need overnight delivery of avocadoes in July, when they tend to spoil fast? No problem.

Burt realized, of course, that however nimble he was, he couldn't compete on efficiencies of scale with the big refrigerated truckers – companies like C.R. England and Swift Refrigerated – that could always underbid him. His father never worried about them because he wasn't after their customers. But Burt was. He hired another team to make the case to small shippers that merger was the only survival strategy. His vision, which kept evolving, was to retain some of their management. He'd also retain their best drivers.

Nor did he stop with trucking. He contracted with rail lines that handled refrigerated containers. He saw an opening beyond his original tri-state market. "I had to adapt to reality" he told me. Reality is inter-modal." His father hated containers because they all looked alike. "How does anyone keep track of them?" he'd ask Burt. Now Burt knew where every container was, 24/7. "If you've got the technology," he said, "you'll never lose a single banana."

But Burt knew that if he was ever to rival the C.R. Englands of this world, he'd have to look like he could. He joined industry groups. He gave talks. He published a newsletter filled with his views on regulation, workplace safety, and the demand for climate-friendly refrigerants. He rented new office space.

When the pandemic hit, Burt saw his biggest opening. Refrigerated carriers were suddenly visible and indispensable. "We were suddenly popular! Everyone loved us, including private equity." Burt adapted by going into capital markets with a gusto that he never could previously have displayed. With a team that he put together from the smaller companies he had acquired, he developed a business plan that would attract investors. It called for steady acquisition of more small firms, while continuing to upgrade technology.

Of course, Burt had to allow a couple of the private equity guys onto his board, but he understood that he was no longer running a family operation. Part of adapting to reality is letting go of old, comfortable models for those that are open to new possibilities. If the private equity guys squelch some of his initiatives, his job – as he saw it – was to help them adapt as well. Burt was essentially fearless. Not impetuous, but convinced that if he put in the work and exercised his imagination, he'd bring other people along with him. After all, it was in everyone's interest – including his financiers' – to allow him to succeed.

Will Burt ever rival the multi-billion-dollar behemoths? He's still got time. The point is that he has a profound understanding of how it might be done. So, think about this:

- Burt did not hesitate to get down in the weeds, and immerse himself in the details of his business – a great leader is hardly above-it-all. Visions are real, tangible things, not airy ideals.
- People who run aspects of your business will likely know more about those aspects than you do. Do you know enough to remain credible with them, and to inspire their confidence?
- Are your questions targeted, so that people know what you want? You don't want to frustrate people with vague, open-ended queries that may yield anomalous results.

Burt's story demonstrates that having a vision means executing a series of detailed plans. Do you give yourself and others the chance to do that? Leaders can't afford to be impatient. They are also adept at keeping a dozen balls in the air at once, and making sure that they all hit the ground in the right order. Some problems depend for their solution on solving other problems. Knowing when you're ready to tackle the next problem is crucial, and that knowledge comes from understanding the depth of a problem and its ramifications throughout the rest of the operation. How do you do that? By consultation with your teams and by developing a deep understanding of what they know. If teams think they can get away with doing less, they may be tempted. Don't let them even think of it. You should talk their language, gain their confidence, even inspire their admiration. You should ask the kind of questions that suggest you could probably provide a pretty good answer on your own.

Finally, it's crucial to encourage your teams to feel like they're part of your vision, i.e., that they're making it happen. They should care about whether you succeed, and are entitled to expect proper credit. Remember, you're not an island – so don't act like one. Actually, part of your role as a leader is to promote communication among teams. So, determine how their tasks intersect, and facilitate useful in-person connections. Think of your teams as forming a living Venn Diagram, where your project is central but all the interscting parts define the center. So, keep the conversation going and pay attention.

I've talked about how a vision can evolve, and how we must evolve to accommodate it. Over time, there's a give-and-take, so that what we see for ourselves – as it slowly, even painfully comes into focus – gets into sync with how we work on ourselves to achieve it. Along the way, we can't expect total clarity. We may even ask fundamental questions about whether we are up to the task and, even more fundamentally, whether what we are trying to achieve is right for us. In other words, questions will arise as to who we are, and who we want to be, which only we can answer. No one else can do our introspection for us, no one else has our imagination. So, my point, which is the basis for this next story, is that setting out to make a vision a reality requires that we understand what motivates us, what really makes us tick.

In becoming a leader, we need to be confident that that's what we really want.

Here, my client must negotiate two competing visions for her life. One entails leadership, one does not. How does she reconcile them? She must determine whether to take up the challenge – which she never sought – by determining whether it is personally right for her, given her other personal goals.

What's interesting, however, is that even here a personal struggle entails the intervention of so many other people. They all feel entitled to consideration. As my client comes around to accepting the challenge, she discovers that even determining who she is may not be so intimate a decision as she might have imagined. As we have already seen, a vision is rarely just our own. Nevertheless, we need to be comfortable with it. It needs to be sufficiently our own so that we can commit to it.

Pursuing a vision requires a delicate balance. In this case, the woman in our story sets out to find this balance. Not without some soul-searching, and with a lot of help. So, as you read her story, ask yourself:

- *Am I an accidental leader, who more or less fell into the role? If so, what practical and psychological work must I do to a) accept the role with enthusiasm or b) definitively reject it?*
- *Whom do I trust to advise me?*
- *Is leadership in one area of my life compatible with my other roles?*

Very few roles in life are forever. If you accept a leadership role, there is no shame in finally concluding that it is not for you. On the other hand, you might find out that it suits you, or that you gain valuable experience. It's worthwhile asking people who have done similar things, and made the role their own. Leadership roles are malleable, and we should not be afraid of their becoming some rigid, all-encompassing prison. Nor should we be afraid that they will make the rest of our lives impossible. A leader remains in control of how their vision affects their life.

Thus, while leadership is always more than just a job, it need not be totally tranformative. You will still have a personal life outside your role – much depends on how much you give to that role. If you can get the job done in a reasonable amount of time with a reasonable level of effort, then you are in he clear. Worrying and obsessinf over what a leaership role will do to your life – how it will change your relationships and sense of self – is pointless until you have embarked on it. Save your stress for when you actually begin to lead.

Finding Your Vision, Finding Yourself

To Lead, You Should Be Comfortable with Making a Commitment to Lead

Lee faced the issue of what she really wanted. In her late twenties she was from a traditional family with deep roots in New York's Chinatown. That enclave, like its "satellites" in Brooklyn and Queens, was never primarily a draw for tourists. Mostly, it's inward-looking, still concerned with preserving inherited cultural institutions. Walk down some streets on a weekday, and you forget the surrounding city. Signs are in Chinese, children chatter in Mandarin. Women wear the cheongsam. The place feels remarkably insular – but homey to those who belong there. Lee told me, "It's comfortable. You know everybody, and you want to stay." She understood that she'd marry a Chinese-American, probably from among her classmates at Hunter College, and then settle down in one of the close-packed apartment buildings to raise a family.

Life only started getting complicated when a building she'd had her eye on during college became a topic of conversation around the dinner table. Her father owned the building. It was one of several that he owned in Chinatown and in the outer boroughs, catering to the Chinese diaspora. He had built his little "empire" with his brother – their forebears were laborers – but then suddenly, when Uncle Charlie had a stroke, her father felt overburdened. "Someone else needs to run the back office," he told her, "or I'll have to sell that building you like. It's all too much for me." Out of a sense of duty, Lee switched her major from Art to Business, and started working for her father evenings and weekends. When she graduated, she became his administrator, making sure the rents were paid, the contractors were paid, and the buildings were up to code. "I convinced my fiancée," she told me, "that we should postpone having kids while I helped my family."

Now, six years later and still "postponing" a family, Lee was unsure whether the path that she was on – towards inevitable leadership of a small but demanding family business – was where she ought to be. Her values were in conflict: she was raised to be a wife and mother, but also with a strong commitment to family. "My father provides decent housing for our community. How can I let him down, or let my neighbors down?" She knew that if some developer bought up the family's real estate, the buildings would be gutted, becoming yet another factor in gentrifying ethnic communities all over the city. So, if she stayed on her trajectory, she would not just lead a business . . . she'd be a civic leader ("My father is holding off the Millennials."), with all the ensuing exposure and demands on her time.

As we began to talk, I sensed that Lee was struggling. "Don't you think that having a family is compatible with running a business?" I asked. Her husband, who was now anxious to start a family, had asked the same question, though he recognized Lee's commitment to her father and community, and wanted her to resolve the issue in her own mind – at least for a while, anyway. I wasn't sure whether, if Lee stayed in the business, her marriage might ultimately suffer. She knew she had to resolve the issue, but she also kept thinking up ways to defer an honest resolution.

She would cut things down the middle. "I see myself," she said, "as a neo-traditionalist. I'm helping my father, but setting myself up to lead a business." In her community, women rarely assumed roles traditionally held by men. The only problem was that, however she spun staying at the firm, she still saw it as keeping her from being a proper, traditional mother. "If you can bend tradition when it comes to leadership," I suggested, "why not bend it with regard to motherhood?" I really did think that she could do both, provided she got sufficient help with the business and with any children she might have.

We talked for a while about coming to terms with who one wanted to be, not in some ideal all-or-nothing sense, but in terms of one's actual life. "We all want to be some ideal, perfect embodiment of something," I said, "but how many people do you know who actually are?" I thought that if she could see her way to becoming both a businesswoman/civic leader and a mother, she would have fewer grounds for regret than if she just chose one over the other. I asked her to think about who and what she wanted to be in terms that were less absolute. I asked whether she saw a way to embrace tradition amply – rather than in some narrow way – by redefining it relative to her own immediate, personal context.

"It has to feel right to you, but you won't really know until you think things through based on all your resources, all your means of support." So, we embarked on a process of thinking about how Lee could be comfortable in both worlds. Could she recognize herself as someone who breaks out of the mold but, still, not so completely that it lies in unrecognizable pieces all around her?

Lee spoke with her husband who, as an employee at a tech start-up, worked crazy hours but also had flexibility. He had never wanted her to be a clone of her mother and grandmother (so he said), and would pitch in when kids came along. Of course, I suspected that no matter what his real feelings regarding diapers, he was so happy to head off a showdown over children that he readily agreed to taking up any domestic slack. He also observed that many young families in Chinatown had amahs for their children, which they could afford with two incomes. He knew Lee, and knew that she might feel self-conscious if she weren't always seen to be with her children, teaching them to be bi-lingual. "'If they have Chinese amahs,' he told her, 'everyone will know that you're bringing them up to be at home in Chinese culture.'" He was a bright guy and, obviously, was intent on getting her wheels turning.

If Lee was ever going to want a leadership position, it had to seem natural, not like some superimposition that would interfere with her instincts, and with her experience of herself in the culture she respected. The challenge was whether she could be a mother, and still satisfy herself that she was adhering to her values of good, traditional mothering. We spoke about how no one expected her to ignore her values, or even substantially to redefine them. What people would understand, and what she might bring herself to understand, was that when values collide – as they had in her case – there was room for honest compromise. As it turned out, her father (who was even more traditional than she was) was so anxious for grandchildren that he offered to pay for the amah if she'd stay in the business. "Apparently," she told me, "amahs are less expensive than hiring someone to replace me. It also turns out that my father wants to keep the business in the family." If her father was willing to compromise, how could she refuse to?

Nonetheless, I am not sure how Lee will work out her issues. But I think she now realizes that before we embark on a leadership role, we must understand – and accept – how it fits into our vision for the rest of our lives. It must somehow feel integral. This entails examining who we think we are, how far we are willing to change, and whether those around us can share our vision. We can stop being absolutist with ourselves when we stop attributing unrealistic, demanding absolutism to others (they have their own issues too). In any event, we can go a long way before giving up on some core sense of who we are and should be. Leadership brings its own rewards that can be consistent with a vision of who we want to become. Lee wants to help her family and community. If she asks herself the right questions and finds real, practicable answers, she can be the leader that her family and community need even while she respects her values. These questions might include:

- What are my essential values, and how does a leadership role require that I compomise them – now and in the medium term?
- Can I find a work-around that allows for some compromise, but still allows me to feel useful, honest, even dutiful to others who depend on me?
- Are other people willing to cut me some slack, and how much can I ask of them? Whose feelings do I really care about?

Everyday Leaders must often ask themselves questions about their role that implicate their family and community. They have to decide how much time, energy, and consideration to give to the concerns of each. So, be prepared for a balancing act that may require detailed explanations. You will need to live with those explanations for a while, so think them through thoroughly. While you can always reverse a decision to lead, you do not want ot hurt anyone before or after.

Lee's story demonstrates the need to be psychologically ready to lead. Think of it in terms of how a Method actor prepares for a role – they try to understand it thoroughly so they can interpet it within their range of skills. They get inside the character's head. They imagine themselves *as* the character, and are psychologically prepared to *be* the character on stage. This takes time. Stanislavski's famous book on acting is, appropriately, called *An Actor Prepares* (1936). Lee came to grips with the psychological component of her role, and realized how prominent it was. As you pursue your own vision, you should accept the psychological component of pursuing it. You may have to ask yourself some hard personal questions. It's part of the role.

Some people just know, early on, that they want (or need) to be leaders in some area of commercial or civic life (think of Burt). For them, the question is how to get there, given their own unique challenges. They struggle, of course, and their concept of leadership may evolve over the trajectory of their personal growth. But very early in their careers, they know that some form of leadership is right for them. That is, their vision of themselves is founded in taking charge, and in directing a group that is larger than themselves. These people have the "leadership gene," a drive to run things that is sufficiently credible to themselves so that, once they begin to pursue their vision, they never look back. They're naturals. If they had applied to West Point, it would have been in character.

But what about the other people, the ones who never dreamed of becoming a leader but somehow find themselves in that position? How did that happen? How did they suddenly surprise themselves, and everybody else?

We saw how Lee tentatively, reluctantly, and with some gentle pressure finally moved into (or towards) leadership. Once she did, she grasped the opportunity, but never quite so much as to entirely forsake her other competing motivations. In the story that follows, however, a woman initially has no idea that she wants to be a leader. But then POW! She gets a taste for it and just keeps building on her skills and opportunities. In effect, she discovers that she can lead, not least because she loves it.

She presents a different profile from people who know early on that they're destined to lead. This type of self-discovery is more common among women, especially those who have lived a comfortable life in a traditional setting.

We learn from this woman's story that it's never too late. We can catch up fast. We also learn not be defensive about wanting to lead once we discover that we do – instead, it's okay to go for it. No need to be self-conscious. A vision is no less authentic because it has only recently grabbed us. If a vision presents itself (anytime), that is reason enough. The idea that we must justify pursuing a vision as far as we can is socially counter-productive.

As you read this story, ask yourself:

- *Do I enjoy making things happen as I think they should, ideally happen? This is a basic leadership trait, and an indication that you may be leadership material.*
- *Am I ready for a new challenge? Often, we reach a point in life where everything seems predictable as far out as we can imagine, and some new undertaking might kick us into high gear.*
- *Does leadership merely sound ineresting, or am I ready to expend the effort? Leaders are not dilettants. Leaderhip is serious. People will depend on you.*
- *Is there a project that I'd like to lead, and am I pepared to do what it takes to take charge? Be specific, be honest.*

Leaderhip roles can arise suddenly. We may even feel blindsided by them. But when confronted, your fight-or-flight instinct may not necessarily lead you in the right direction. Maybe you want to stop, hold your ground, and think things through. Much will depend on whether you like your vision enough to give yourelf to it. Half-hearted pursuits go nowhere, and only waste everyone's time. So, find out as much as you can – about the potential project and about yourself. Nothing needs to happen all at once, so long as your progress is thought through and steady enough to bolster your confidence.

Do you remember, when you were three feet tall, how your parents made nicks on the door-jamb every time you grew an inch? The analogy may seem infantilizing now, but in principle it's useful. You got <u>excited</u> as you grew. Seeing your progres was encouraging. So, as you start out in leadership, it's helpful to keep a record of what you achieve – maybe in a dedicated diary, maybe on a spreadsheet. You can literally track how you're doing – i.e., how many new customers, new leads, new hires. In effect, you can make your own case for becoming a *leader. If you remain unconvinced, well, at least you'll have evidence (provided, of course, that your timetable is reasonable).*

Discovering Leadership

Once You Find Your Vision, then Give it All You Have!

In returning to work after a hiatus, Ellen discovered that she wanted – and had the capacity – to become an industry leader. All she had initially desired was decent work but, in performing it, it was if a recessive leadership gene expressed itself. Her story demonstrates how each of us, minding our own business, needs to be open to our leadership potential. If natural leaders always believe in themselves, the rest of us should at least be able to recognize our potential to lead and then make the most of it. We might suffer if we blithely turn away, too caught up in the day-to-day to jump-start our potential. We could feel as though we never became who we should have been. Sometimes, we need to lead just to hold onto what we have.

When Ellen came to see me, she had three school-age children and a rich husband. She'd been "a Mother with a capital M" (her term) for several years, but now that all the kids were in school she needed to keep busy. So, she had returned to teaching middle school English. But it rankled. "To be honest," she said, "after round-the-clock babysitting, I'm not looking for an *in loco parentis* position. I want to be out in the world." I've heard this before. Women finally liberated from caring for children crave involvement with grown-ups. But the transition is hard. I wasn't sure what Ellen could do – did she have any transferable skills?

As an English teacher she could presumably write well, so I suggested PR. "You'd be amazed at how few people can write," I told her. But Ellen outdid me. "You know," she said, "contacts trump talent. My sister is a real estate agent and knows everybody." She knew she could at least get an interview – which she did. Better yet, she was hired as an apprentice agent.

Over the next several months. Ellen passed the state and national real estate licensing exams. She became an associate agent. What I hadn't expected (and perhaps she hadn't either), was that real estate would consume her. She threw herself into it. She made deals, and on two occasions was the firm's highest performing broker. "You know," she told me, "I've fallen in love with this business. It's like I've found my true calling." Apparently, clients loved her, and the love-fest became intoxicating. I wondered if we had anything more to talk about.

But we did. She wanted to buck the whole thing up a notch. I thought of Mae West's line, TOO MUCH OF A GOOD THING CAN BE WONDERFUL. Apparently, Ellen wanted to run the whole shop, or at least be an equal partner with the guy who ran it. Would he be interested? Did she have the equity to invest the firm? More fundamentally, was she prepared to take on a leadership role? There were a dozen or so associate agents, and she'd have to manage them all – not just her own portfolio. She'd have to become a businesswoman, as well as a player in local politics (by which real estate lived or died). She was, she said, entirely up for it. She couldn't imagine anything better.

As Ellen got into the game, she discovered her *need* to be a leader. "I know what it takes to sell high-end properties," she told me. "It takes staging, and technology, and a Ph.D. in psychology or its moral equivalent." The guy who ran the firm was intransigently old-school, and Ellen felt he was holding her back. "The only way to get ahead is to lead," she said. "It's what I need." In a few months, she pulled it off.

In fact, not only did she become partner – with an infusion of equity capital from her husband – but she ultimately bought the guy out. The firm was hers. She could make all the changes she wanted. Ellen couldn't stop talking. I thought she'd finally got what she wanted.

Wrong again. Once someone discovers the prerogatives of leadership – the power to make things happen – it can kick off an infinite feed-back loop. Leadership can make you want to lead bigger groups, and make even more things happen. Ellen opened satellite offices, and hired more brokers. She wanted to have the biggest independent brokerage in the county. She started speaking at women's groups, the local realtors' association, even at synagogues (in the latter instance, under the rubric of helping retirees conserve their capital). I wondered what was driving her – was it insecurity, some narcissistic need to show off, a keen sense of business, or just the rush of seeing her name on all the "For Sale" signs and being in charge of a huge operation?

According to Ellen, it was all the above, but also the thrill of getting in touch with what she considered her real motivations. "I guess I was the perfect wife and perfect mother," she said, "but those are roles that women inherit. On the other hand, when you take control of something, and grow it and make it better – when you make it your own – then that's organic." In effect, Ellen was on a mission of self-discovery, pushing the limits of how far she could take her new role. It was therapy-by-other-means.

As Ellen brought in more capital, and merged with another local firm, I wondered when enough would be enough. If once she had proven that she could be a leader, wasn't she just proving the same thing again and again? I thought this high that Ellen was on might be something of an addiction. But Ellen didn't see it that way. She felt that leaders have a need to continually be creative, and that *that* was where she was. "I am discovering myself as a creative, much as an artist would who picks up a brush and sees that she can paint. This is all about discovering who I am, not about taking over the world." In Ellen's estimation, leadership was ostensibly outer-facing, but it was also an inward journey. "Maybe men are into power," she said, "but even they must need to experience themselves through what they create."

With another woman, Ellen started a real estate academy dedicated to educating the next generation of female realtors. She told me that she had flocks of applicants – proof, she said, that her own leadership had inspired others to take a similar journey. I had to admit she was probably right.

Ellen discovered that she was a natural leader. She had the gene. Her story demonstrates that not only can someone evolve into a leader because of necessity; they can discover that leadership is highly compatible with the person they would have wanted to be in the first place, if only they had understood how they would take to it. So, the point is to hold yourself open to the possibility. If you feel the urge to take the reins of an organization, perhaps that urge comes naturally. You can feel entitled to follow it. If you are like Ellen, you may find that it opens up competencies that you didn't know you had. You may find that it opens you up to who you really are.

If you don't follow through, you may be angry at yourself later on. Why risk it? While Ellen's story may seem like an over-the-top indulgence of someone with money behind her, it is also a model adaptable to anyone's circumstances. At her academy, Ellen has a sign over the door: "You owe it to yourself to try." In a benign reversal of *The Godfather*, she insists it's strictly personal, not business.

So, as you reflect on Ellen, try to engage in some what-if, alternative history: what would happen if I didn't follow the urge to lead and then take it to the max? Would I always be apologizing to myself? Would I feel like I let myself down? If you can honestly say that your life would be less satisfying, and that you'd always regret a missed opportunity, then the risk to your self-esteem – should you fail – is worth it. Not much in life comes without a cost.

Notice, however, that Ellen did not just take a leap of faith into a new career. She started as an apprentice, passed the exams, and worked her way up. *Real leaders, even born leaders, do not necessarily start at the top.* They become acclimated, learning the language and culture. They learn the ropes. Like Ellen, they cultivate the right contacts – people who they work with synergistically. At some point, Ellen ceased to surprise herself. She felt she was on a limitless trajectory. But it took time and constant reinforcement. So, take account of your own progress. Are you on the upswing, however gentle the curve? If so, then you are probably moving in the right direction, and drawing on your natural skills.

We've talked about finding experts to help make your vision a reality. We've talked about building them into teams. But there is another permutation of this approach: building networks of people who know what they're doing (even if they're not "experts") whom you can call on when you need support.

Everyone knows about networking. The term usually appears in connection with looking for a job (LinkedIn, anyone?). But networks have other uses. They allow us to expand our reach. They can act as our proxies. They can join a project that we cannot pursue on our own. They can be cogs in the wheels of a vision that cannot roll along solely on our personal power.

In this expanded context, networks are groups of people who do things with us and for us just because they're there. A leader knows how to create such networks, and use them effectively. Some leaders could never imagine having arrived at their positions except by virtue of the networks surrounding them.

In this story, a young man first discovers the utility of experts and then – crucially – discovers how to multiply his effectiveness through networking. He creates an entire business model based on networking. But rather than being the sole beneficiary, he allows the benefits to circulate through the network. This is where he displays a touch of genius. Who, after all, wants to be of service (at least for an extended period) without participating in the value proposition? This young man turns the network into a machine for distributing mutual benefits.

We can all create networks that support our vision. But we must design them so that people want to remain committed. My client first learned that he needed experts, and then teams; then he discovered that networks are not just like teams – they're more loosely organized and, ultimately, based not only on skills but on being available when those skills become crucial. They are immensely useful, provided there is incentive enough for them to remain functional.

So, as you read this story, think about these issues:

- *Are you a skilled networker? Do you know how to get people excited about joining your network and contributing what they know?*
- *Are you able, like my client, to make networking fun – as much of an adventure for the network's members as for you?*
- *Does your vision include aggregating talent around you INFORMALLY, to be called on (and rewarded) when you need it?*
- *Have you figured out how to reward people, and keep them involved, by offering growth potential?*

My client would be able to answer these questions with a Yes. He was an instinctive networker. But it's a skill you can learn. Don't be shy about putting yourself out there. Have your elevator pitch ready. Make the possibilities seem plausible (not by misrepresentation, but by displaying your knowledge of an untapped market). Let people know they're a valuable resource, and encourage them to share your vision. Above all, be able to spot talent aligned with ambition. People do not need to become formal employees if they can help grow your operation and participate in its success.

Experts And Networks

Leaders Need External Networks – Not Just Internal Teams – to Deal with Problems Effectively

Successful entrepreneurs love their origin stories. Dave traces his success back to a lemonade stand, which he started when he was eight and which (so he claims) revolutionized lemonade sales on street corners in New Jersey. One day,

I asked Dave why he kept recurring to his earliest entrepreneurial feats when, right now, his business was orders of magnitude larger and more complicated. "Why?" he asked. "Because you learn from the beginning what you need to do, and then you keep doing it instinctively." What he meant, was that basic experiences are formative. We just keep building on them. For a business person, a vision becomes real as he or she applies what they've learned to the next challenge. In the context of leadership, they *learn* how to lead so that – when the time comes – they can make the right move fast, with confidence.

So, as to Dave's lemonade stand . . . he'd sell about 50 cups on a good day. But customers sometimes crossed the street to the Puerto Rican lady, who sold "limber do coco" (frozen ice pops made from coconut milk). Dave realized that however cold he made his lemonade, her treats were colder. What could he do?

Dave consulted his first expert, his mother.

She told him that you couldn't just freeze lemonade and sell it, since there would be no way to eat it (except by waiting for a melt-down – a slow, messy process, attractive to flies). You could make slushies, but they'd have to be served at once and their volume would pose a challenge (you could never carry around gallons of the stuff all day). "So, why not offer lemonade pops?" she asked him. "You could keep them on dry ice, and they'd be perfect." A lightbulb lit up in Dave's head.

But it wasn't the lightbulb you might think. In one of our sessions, Dave told me that the first lesson in business that he learned was the value of experts. "My mother knew a lot about pops. She'd never made them, but she understood the concept." Dave learned, at age eight, that when you can't solve a problem, you find people who can – and then you take their advice. Dave's mother (now made co-director of the stand) said they'd have to buy popsicle molds, and that she'd advance him the money (repayable out of his profits at a standard rate of interest). Once they read the directions on the molds, Dave and his mother experimented with recipes, since you needed a certain amount of milk or yogurt to give the pops body. Dave practiced how to use the molds, and how to unmold the pops so that they stayed firm.

"I was so excited when I rolled out my new product line," he told me. "I gave people a choice – lemonade or popsicles. My sales went way up." Dave and his mother continued to experiment with limeade pops and raspberry pops (Dave got raspberries at the farmer's market, which his mother squished in the blender.) "You see," he told me, "once you find an expert, you can access their expertise – and bring it along as your business grows." The lesson stayed with Dave, he said, and he was proud of how he'd applied it.

When he started his next business in college, Dave was selling t-shirts. "I had this vision that I could get rich before I even graduated, scaling up my sales to a hundred colleges. It was like how I multiplied selling popsicles." Dave's model was that anyone could upload a photo of an image, and Dave would print it on the shirt. Fifteen years ago, the idea was novel. Dave advertised in the student paper, and people responded. "But then I came up with my next insight. When I hit the wall with ads, I needed to network." Dave recruited his friends at other colleges into his "network."

He made t-shirts for these friends at no cost, and asked them to wear the shirts. When someone inquired "Where'd you get that?" (which, invariably, they did), the friend would explain the procedure (for a cut of the profits, of course). "What I learned," Dave told me, "was that you can't depend solely on yourself. In a way, hiring an expert and relying on your network are two sides of the same coin – they extend you beyond yourself." By the time Dave graduated, he had sales at over a hundred campuses. Word had spread. But it started with Dave's networking initiative. Dave had become a leader in the field of print-to-order t-shirts. He finally sold his company to one of the employees.

Of course, you hear all the time that networking is a key to success. But Dave told me that until he'd actually relied on it, he'd been skittish. "I was a little embarrassed, and I had to get used to it." That is, he had to make the practice feel routine. "After a while, I found that networking works both ways – I'd ask, they'd ask, it was all part of getting ahead." The point is that Dave had to learn how to live (and operate) in a networked world, so that as he made his subsequent, big-time moves, networking felt natural. "What I was after," he said, "was a network of experts. I wanted people who could *do* stuff, but mostly who really *knew* stuff."

After college, Dave got his chance. He opened a micro-distillery, which was written up in *Whiskey Afficionado*. Of course, he knew nothing about making whiskey, but he hired guys who did. He made friends among other small distillers in the area and, when he decided that the business was too small to compete nationally, he called on the network of distillers he'd established to help him find a buyer. "I loved that business," he told me, "but my ambitions outgrew its potential." Then he added, crucially, "I learned a lot in the five years that I ran it. I was never going to lead the industry, but I learned how to lead a growing company." It was, in effect, a bigger lemonade stand.

Dave had been a small businessman since the lemonade stand, and felt that since then he'd experienced the problems of the species. "Our aspirations are always bigger than our means – but we can find the means by bootstrapping our connections and by knowing where to find the right experts." He wanted to be a leader in the small business space. "Okay, I've always wanted to lead a company. I mean, that's what entrepreneurs do. But if you own a space, or conspicuously co-own it, your company is that much more likely to succeed." Dave was drawing on what he'd learned, not least from distilling, and he sought to apply it in a much more public arena. He was scaling up again in terms of size and of visibility.

He thought that the basic need of all small businesspeople was access to affordable capital. "What if," he said, "there were a network of investors willing to fund small businesses, with the expertise to evaluate the level of risk? You wouldn't have to rely on banks, which are so conservative, or venture capitalists who want to micro-manage you." Then he went a step further. "What if the investors were other small businesses, too small to diversify into other fields, but big enough to lend money at competitive rates?" It sounded interesting. We discussed how he would pull it off and how, if the venture were successful, he would profit along with the investors.

Dave had to incorporate his service, of course, and then hire a lawyer, an accountant, and several analysts – all of them experts! – who could evaluate the risks of potentially eligible companies. He would put together a group of companies that qualified for capital, and another that could invest. His role was to make the introductions, backed up by solid analysis. For the service, he knew he'd need the right kind of experts. Also, he'd need to call on his network of friends, several of whom were now on Wall Street. "But mostly," he told me, "I am not just using my network, but creating a new, synergistic network." He hoped that it would become self-perpetuating, as some companies swung from needing capital to wanting to invest in still more companies that needed capital.

In effect, Dave understood that:

- As we begin to lead, we need all sorts of support – the rights teams, specific experts, and various networks that we can call on as the need arises.
- He should give talent a stake in the outcome of his projects – their commitment to him would also be a commitment to themselves.

Dave exemplifies how we learn from the ground up in business, learning to see what we don't know, learning to call on people who can help us. As he points out, experts are just the flip-side of our network, i.e., they're all people we learn to call on as we assume a leadership role. Currently, Dave's company has profits of over $10 million annually. He has his sights on the next big thing. His vision, so to speak, is wide-angled. But he thinks he knows how to achieve it.

As you reflect on this story, recall that Dave started small. His networking grew in tandem with his business' growth. He never got ahead of himself – either in networking or entrepreneurially. He regarded the two as necessary to each other. It's tempting to build up a network before you have much to offer, but such networks are unlikely to hold if only because you *don't* have much to offer. People will provide their talents when they see (or can plausibly project) a pay-off. So, as your business grows, you should put together surrounding players who will help it continue growing. Needs will become apparent, and you should become astute at identifying them. As in Burt's case, you'll need to get down in the weeds. You'll also need to act opportunely, while what you can offer is still attractive and before the talent goes elsewhere. It's not easy, but it can be exciting.

Most of the time, we regard a vision as "our" vision, something that "we" pursue. It's ego-driven, an element of our unique take on our own life. But wait! Nobody goes through life on a straight track that never crosses anyone else's. We all run into each other all the time. To the extent that each person has a separate vision, those visions are destined to collide, almost kaleidoscopically, so that finally our personal visions are inflected with those of everyone else. In effect, any one person's vision becomes an aspect of other people's.

When we set out to realize our vision, we must accept that it will be influenced, in some cases even transformed, by those other people. In this sense, we don't own our vision. In the best of circumstances, it becomes a collaboration. We should be willing to let go, listen, and share our imagination of who we think we should be. From this perspective, leadership becomes a negotiation. We work towards what we hope to achieve, even as we share with other people what that should be and how we should get there.

Sharing a vision does not diminish it. Rather, it means that we live in the real world. In the realm of the real, we bring people on board with our vision, even as we compromise, and take account of their life experience. Is this a deflection? No. If we want to get anywhere, we need to operate through other people's goodwill, understanding, expertise, and sense that their own aspirations are as valid as our own.

Of course, in the process our vision may be altered. But think of it this way: isn't any straight-ahead version of reality altered when we add peripheral vision? Ultimately, it's the difference between what's in front of our face and the complete, complicated picture that encompasses all sides of what's out there. We know more. We see other possibilities. We're better able to assess the risks of our next likely moves. Taking account of other people's wishes as we realize our own is not only necessary; it makes good sense. We should be willing to work in tandem. The best leaders always do.

In this story, a young man discovers the necessity of opening his vision to the scrutiny of others. He is allowed to lead when they decide that he is willing to share some of their vision, and incorporate it into his own. He becomes an embodiment of the collectivity that he leads, even as he provides a type of guidance that is always up for debate. Is this leadership in the way, say, Ellen or Dave would define it? Probably not. But it is what is called for under the circumstances, i.e., where any leader who is not straight down the middle is likely to be challenged.

This guy plays the long game. By indirection, he finds direction out (to paraphrase Hamlet's speech). We see a type of leadership that some of us might not even consider except if we have lots of patience – and maybe, even, a degree of desperation. But looked at in its most favorable light, this type of almost crab-like leadership, moving from side to side while it inches along, demonstrates commitment.

Having a vision and wanting to achieve it may mean bending to other people's will. But it does not mean breaking. Leaders do no always get just what they want exactly when they want it. But that is reason enough to hold oneself out as an inspiration, so that (along the way) others can appreciate your vision and want to support it.

As you read this story, ask yourself:

- *Am I willing to accept other people's ideas, and even alter my vision accordingly, in order to roughly approximate where I'd like to go?*
- *Can I evaluate others' ideas objectively, from an array of perspectives, or am I so involved with my own ideas that I'm incapable of being objective?*
- *Are my give-and-take skills adequate when dealing with a personal vision that means a lot to me, and even reflects on my self-estimation?*
- *Can I accept that working with others, and giving their ideas a shot, will make achieving my vision a longer-term proposition? If I can't, is this based on personal need rather than cool, detached business judgment?*

Often, our ego demands that we see results – now. They must look like what we we want them to, or we fall into a funk. But when other people are involved in executing our vision, our ego nust take a step back. Maybe someone has a legitimate point or, at least, a stake in the outcome that we cannot dismiss. In these instances, timing is not of the essence. We need to listen, and make a deliberate show of acknowledging their advice (which we may see as closer to a demnd). This may require altering our vision. But remember, just as we seek to protect our vision, other people have interests that they want to protect. It's a negotiation. No leader is an island. No leader inhabits a vacuum. So now, watch as Dov collides with reality, and then accepts that he has to deal with it.

A Vision In A Kaleidoscope

Moving Ahead, Leaders Allow Other People to Share Their Vision and Shape it

Consider Dov, who had to learn (the hard way) how to share his vision. When he first came to see me, Dov was a rabbi without a congregation – after five years at a local shul, his contract had lapsed. "They said I was too progressive," he told me, "and in Orthodox circles that's the kiss of death. I wanted to attract young professional women, and the Sisterhood rebelled." Dov thought that building a religious community required constant renewal, even if fundamental religious beliefs remained constant. Apparently, his congregation was happier with a smaller, more uniform membership. "My vision was for a bigger tent," he said. "But they were still out in the desert with their own little tribe." Dov thought he could resurrect his vision at another congregation – but could he?

Unlike most Orthodox Jews, let alone most Orthodox rabbis, Dov was divorced. He and his wife had split up just after he lost his job. Almost a year later, he'd found no congregation willing to talk to him beyond an initial interview. "It's like you need a rebbetzin," he said. "Marriage gives you gravitas and, besides, congregations want a team." It sounded plausible, but I wondered whether there wasn't something more. "Maybe they just see you as that guy who wants to disrupt things."

What I meant, of course, was that perhaps Dov was so committed to his own vision of community-building that he scared people. Nobody *wants* a leader who doesn't acknowledge the feelings of people that he leads. So, I suggested that the next time he had an interview, he should emphasize that while change is inevitable, he would be open to adjusting the pace, even the scope of change, so that people remain comfortable. "Present yourself as a leader with good ideas who welcomes everyone's ideas on how they should be realized." The point was not to forsake his vision of community building, so much as to recognize that we never lead in a vacuum. People are all around us, and we have to address their wishes. "Think about it," I said. "By its nature a 'community' is a shared space – community-building is a shared enterprise, and you should convey that you know that."

Dov waited for his next interview, this time disposed to be tractable.

The interview came from a small Sephardic congregation, which approached him because there was a shortage of Sephardic rabbis. Or, at least, that was the only explanation that Dov could offer, since he was obviously an Ashkenazi (that is, Dov was from a European tradition while Sephardi were mostly Middle Eastern). "I think they were open-minded enough to listen," he told me, "but I wondered how far I'd get." Sephardim tend to be insular. In this case, many spoke halting English. Some spoke only Farsi. "I thought we'd conduct the interview in Biblical Hebrew," he joked. In fact, he wasn't that far off.

Dov sat around a table with some men (all men!), many of whom had immigrated in the '70s and '80s. The others were all first-generation. They were committed to preserving Orthodox tradition but, unlike many Ashkenazim, their cultural ties to their old countries were at least as strong as their religious fervor. Dov could see that the shul was a place of refuge, where they felt safe from an American razmataz that they disliked and made them squirm. "You know," he told me, "they were sort of like Hasidim in business suits. Very out of the ordinary – even for the Orthodox."

So, Dov spoke to them. He (gingerly) laid out ideas to grow the community. He also listened to their ideas, which were less concerned with growth than with maintaining the community as a going concern. "I told them that more members meant more money for projects that they needed – new windows, plumbing, a school – but I realized that I'd have to soft-pedal any membership drive." They didn't want new members who might be culturally anomalous. "I said that we could raise more funds internally, perhaps by expanding the Board. I accepted that 'community-building' is not just adding more people – it can be about preserving tradition." The hope was that people who loved this tradition would find the community. So, in all that Dov told them, he made clear that as a leader he'd work within whatever tolerances that they set out. His leadership would be cooperative.

Dov got the job. He's had it for a couple of years. The Board has expanded, and they've contributed funds. The sanctuary looks nicer. Newly-arrived Sephardi families have started attending services. Dov thinks they will become members if the community offers after-school classes for kids. It's a stretch, another innovation, but Dov will present the idea to the Board in terms of preserving tradition. "If I offer tutoring on my own," he told me, "the parents will likely want to pay me but they won't feel an affiliation to the synagogue itself. I want the Board to understand that." In other words, Dov has learned that he must bring people along with his vision for an expanded, thriving community.

He is aware that things are likely to proceed more slowly than if he could just lead full-throttle with a compliant Board behind him. But the nature of leadership is not always to get out front. You need a sense of the people you are leading: what matters to them, and how can you work with it?

In this sense, leadership is contextual. It operates close to the wind and within established norms. It requires careful calibration, a lot of listening, a sixth-sense sensitivity to what reassures people so that they're unfazed by something new. This type of leadership appreciates the long game. It recognizes that even when there are acute problems – like the windows at Dov's shul – you cannot just swoop in and get them fixed. Dov had to raise the money by expanding the Board so that *then* he could fix the windows. He had to attract new members by offering Hebrew classes in the name of tradition. He accepts the indirectness of it all.

"You wouldn't run a company like this," he told me recently. "But this isn't a company." Dov understands where he is. Of course, the community needs money, but its sense of itself is paramount. Dov's vision, and the leadership he exercises to achieve it, must take account of that. He needs to pursue a shared vision, if he is to lead at all.

Can you be like Dov? Yes, provided you follow some of his moves:

- Dov appreciated that conventional, efficiency-driven principles could not always apply to a style of leadership formulated to serve a specific group with its own principled demands.
- He slowed down, negotiated, presented his ideas in terms that suited his constituency.
- He accepted that change – which was a main driver of his vision – could not be imposed (or seem to be imposed) unilaterally, from the top down. As people got used to the changes, and saw the benefits, they would gradually come around.
- He learned how to draw people towards his vision, appealing to shared interests.

So, if your vision of leadership is to act as a change agent, you will need to consider whom you want to change. To what degree are they amenable? What is their resistance based on, and how can you address it without giving offense?

These are delicate issues. They call for tact. Much of the negotiation is not even verbal. Rather, it operates through subtle acts that have small but positive effects. Openness is key in these situations. You should be a good listener, respectful of every objection. You cannot presume to know better – even when you are confronted with rigidity that seems backward-looking or, at least, uninformed and self-defeating. In such cases, you lead by patience.

***

Each of these leaders pursued a vision that did not come easily – either in its conception or realization. Their stories suggest, therefore, that "having" a vision is too simple a description of the work that goes into pursing what a vision entails. Much of that work involves self-reflection, and the ability to revise a vision as one grows. It involves as well the ability to engage with others who can support one's vision. The process is both inward- and outward-facing. In other words, it's complex. It requires that we be honest with ourselves even as we are acutely aware of the circumstances evolving around us. There needs to be a constant interplay between who we are and where we are.

Obviously, some people are better leaders than others. But, as these stories show, a vision is the necessary starting point – however we ultimately arrive at it. Most of us *are* capable of self-reflection and of responding to circumstances. We can rise to the occasion as, for example, Lee had to do. We are all, therefore, capable of pursuing a vision with a degree of canniness that might come as a surprise once we get started. The point is to sharpen our innate capacities, to learn through experience (of ourselves and the world). None of this is out of reach, provided we make the initial commitment.

Thus, if I were to offer one take-away from this chapter, it would be this:

- Leaders cannot be successful unless they appreciate their environment. They are in constant negotiation with everyone who inhabits it.

Every vision will almost certainly change, as more and more people have their say. We must accept such change, and see it as a type of vitality. Visions are dynamic, as alive as we are. We live with them, just as we live with people who surround us – bumping up aganst challenges, making adjustments, taking on this day and the next. In this sense, the very personal is also political. We must cultivate people skills to pursue a vision, and to make it the basis of any leadership project. Those skills may need to be further honed, based on the specific people whom we seek to lead.

Reference

Stanislavski, Constantin. *An Actor Prepares* (London: Bloomsbury Revelations), 1936/ 2013.

Chapter II

Determination and Flexibility

Just as we should be flexible in defining a vision, we must be flexible as we pursue it. Determination by itself, therefore, is not enough. It must be accompanied by the capacity to respond to change, and to people who do not always support us. This chapter demonstrates how, when we set out to lead, determination and flexibility are two sides of the same coin.

Sometimes, people in leadership positions think (if only to themselves) that "If I got here, I must be doing something right. So why should I compromise?" But, as I will emphasize, that's the best way not to remain a leader. Leaders must retain the loyalty of the led. They must convince people that whatever interests are at stake, are shared – maybe not 50/50, but close enough so that people remain involved, supportive, and willing to weather hard times on the leader's watch. A flexible leader is better able to retain people's trust.

There is a vast literature on how trust develops between people, ranging from intimates to colleagues and employees. But what remains constant is that no one wants to feel unheard, unappreciated, discounted, or even abandoned. Leaders develop trust by listening and displaying empathy. Flexibility arises out of empathy – when we understand how someone feels, and why they feel that way, we can address what they feel are their legitimate needs. We do not have to agree that these needs are justified; they may not be what *we* need; but we should demonstrate concern, and a willingness to take account of what people saying.

Of course, what people do not say may sometimes be more compelling than what they do. The most successful leaders analyze any situation broadly, so that they can take account of a community's norms, its history and social composition. These leaders literally inhabit the place that they seek to lead. In one of the stories that follows, a musician successfully appeals to other musicians because he has literally walked in their shoes – and, to a degree, still does. He understands where they are coming from figuratively but also literally, having come from the same place.

The leaders (and potential leaders) in these stories face obstacles and setbacks. Their progress is non-linear. They get discouraged. But they find enough

DOI: 10.4324/9781003437635-3

in their previous experience to keep going. They understand that they have shown promise in the past, and are capable of personal growth. Perhaps the most important element of determination is a conviction that what we hope to achieve is possible or, at least, that we have the background and psychological mettle to take on the challenge. Of course, we will need energy – but energy is frequently a product of belief in ourselves. Not Pollyanna-ish, naive belief, but a clear-eyed assessment of our own capabilities. Leadership often requires quick-wittedness. We can't stop to ponder if we have the Right Stuff.

We can also give ourselves a boost by finding influential allies. We must learn to interest them in our objectives (even, perhaps, by giving them a stake in our success). As we'll see in the following stories, allies are crucial when we seek to lead a group with an entrenched culture, where members may be skeptical of anyone who represents change.

So, as you read this chapter, think about these issues:

- A leader is prepared to deter opposition before it gets organized. Can you detect emerging challenges, and are you able to put in place a plan to meet them?
- Leaders make their past count in the present – they make the most of what they have. Are you conscious of your experience and transferable skills, and can you readily draw on them?
- Flexibility enhances a leader's credibility – it tells people that you are determined to lead. Are you willing to bend sufficiently? Can you gauge how much bending is sufficient?
- To be flexible, leaders should empathize with those they lead. Can you draw on your work/life experience to develop empathy?
- Leaders make change incrementally, based on what their constituency can tolerate. Are you sensitive to all your stake holders? Do you listen creatively, i.e., do you think while you listen and formulate tactical as well as more long-term responses?
- Are you able to locate influential allies, especially within groups that have their own culture?
- Are you sensitive to cultural factors within groups that you seek to lead?

Leaders are always a step ahead. These are mental steps, since leaders think about how to respond even before the need arises. They make plans. They are always looking around, since it is never possible to know exactly where a challenge will come from. When they sense a challenge, they switch into strategy-mode, deciding how to meet it. But they remain flexible, since no plan is as ineffective as one that is rigid and boxes you in. Yet even at their most determined, great leaders know that unless they understand their challengers, and really know where they're coming from, they won't succeed. Most of the time, such understanding elicits a creative compromise. That's the main point of this chapter.

***

In this story, a young immigrant musician overcomes resistance from her traditional community to a new type of musicality that, while departing from tradition, still features and extends it. She pulls off a kind of balancing act, leading to a new sense of acculturated freedom and personal self-assurance. Her "determination" is in part expressed intellectually, as she constructs arguments to convince more conservative community members that innovation is vital to preserving the fundamental tradition. She advocates a type of cultural openness that is nonetheless non-threatening – if only because she makes it seem natural and organic, a product of the immigrant experience that embodies growth and maturation. She appeals to a desire to put down roots and prosper, even while remaining identifiable as a group (that is, as a group that has retained its cultural integrity).

She also achieves a practical coup, enabling every community member to discover for themselves how exciting a type of new, fusion music can become. She makes her case in real-time performances. She allows the experience of her music to sink in – sensually, spiritually – so that her intellectual arguments seem irrefutable. She puts in the hard work to teach other musicians how to work in her idiom, so that the experience of her new, fusion musicality becomes a fact of local life (and beyond). Ultimately, she makes a career: as an apostle, a performer, and a leader.

This story illustrates how determination can operate on many levels, which finally cohere into a well-coordinated campaign. Determination is inflected by the constituency that a would-be leader hopes to influence. Here, a young musician deployed different types of persuasive techniques based on who was listening, who was making decisions, who might join her in performing. Her overall approach required careful calibration among its various elements. In her case (as in all cases), determination was not just summed up by the will and energy to plow ahead. It was, rather, a careful, well-focused effort that brought together (and found the synergy in) several intelligent tactics.

As you read this story, ask yourself:

- *Do you understand determination to be the application of intense energy to a defined task, or do you see it as a subtler practice that attracts people to your project by appealing to their interests?*
- *Are you culturally sensitive, and aware that what appeals to you and your crowd may offend other people – i.e., that they may have values that you may not understand?*
- *Are you an all-at-once or incremental type person? Are you a competent judge of how much incremental change will succeed, and at what intervals?*
- *Can you pick out the key people who must be brought around if your project is to take off? In other words, have you taken time to understand your constituency and its current influencers?*

Cultural issues are highly sensitive, and an effective leader learns how to navigate them effectively. He or she is never condescending, and recognizes that change may come from a very deep place in someone else's psyche. Even if that person is not afraid of change, they may be afraid to express their willingness. So, it's almost as if consent has to happen across an entire community if it is to happen at all. . . but not necessarily. Leaders know how to find the right people in a community to facilitate what they propose. They can turn these people into credible allies, trusted by the community. Watch how my client does this, and think about how her strategies may apply to you.

Grit

Leaders Use Creativity and Compromise to Deter the Opposition Before it Gets Organized

Elana came to this country when she was three, and in many ways was a typical immigrant. She wanted to fit in, but still felt the tug of her native culture. Her parents fled Iran when the mullahs toppled the Shah. They brought the old traditions with them, and Elana bounced between learning English and singing folk songs in Farsi late at night with the family. She didn't feel conflicted, exactly, but more like two separate people. As a young woman, she wondered whether her public American persona could accommodate her cultural inheritance. "You know," she told me, "I liked being complicated. It just meant that I could do more."

The question was what to do. Her parents, who had fled along with other Jews, had become established in a Persian enclave on Long Island. The children tended to remain in the community – opening businesses, marrying among themselves. But while Elana wanted to maintain close ties with people she had known and loved, she also wanted to break out. "It was like I didn't want to be a clone," she said. "I knew I'd just get angry." She realized *how* angry she would get when a boyfriend suggested that marriage would solve all her problems. "Can you believe that?" she asked me. "I broke up with him, and wondered if they'd all be like that."

But then she got practical. She was a talented musician, and thought she was destined to perform. She studied at Juilliard, and made some recordings. Once, she was a featured soloist at Symphony Space. In her twenties, it seemed that music was her ticket out. Maybe she could tour the world. Lots of musicians did. The problem was that she didn't really want out – at least not entirely. "I wanted to remain close to the community, and I loved my heritage. It was part of me." So, practicality got side-tracked as Elana continued to fret.

I entered the picture about five years ago. Naturally, we spoke about music, and its place in her life. Up until then, music had been what mathematicians call a trap-door problem – easy to pass through in one direction, while it was hard to reverse your steps even slightly. In effect, she could play the classics because she was classically trained, but then she'd *be* a classicist; the door would be pretty well shut on creating another cultural identity. Her musician friends, some of whom were also immigrants, told her how hard it was to keep in touch with their communities when they were touring, and playing what audiences expected to hear.

We tried to formulate a strategy, and here is where Elana's determination – and, ultimately, leadership – started to emerge. For years, she had composed music that fused Persian melodies and techniques with their European (aka classical) counterparts. Her model was the klezmer bands, which updated Jewish folk music with reggae and jazz. They were a hoot, and Elana loved them. They were hardly dignified, however, and Elana saw her own compositions as similar – fun, but not for the concert stage. So, I asked, "Do you have to give concerts? I mean, how about other performance venues?" She had never thought there were venues that could showcase what she called her "secret vice." Could what served as fun for her – a sort of necessary outlet – be of interest to other people, even if not in concert?

Elana determined to find out. Her idea was to engage the Persian community with her music, becoming perhaps a cultural avatar (notwithstanding the community's conservative, self-absorbed, inbred tendencies). She approached the leader of a group that promoted Persian interests on Long Island. It mainly addressed business issues, like zoning and permits, but it also thought of itself as keeping Persian culture alive. Would they go for her? She was not exactly offering what they knew and loved. But she had a pitch: no tradition can survive without acknowledging its new environment, at least somewhat. "I know I was a little over the top," she told me. "But I wanted to make it feel (for them) like life and death." In a way, it was already at that stage for her.

The guy she spoke with was friendly – he knew her parents – but skeptical. He wondered why she had not just pursued her classical career. When she tried to explain, he wondered whether her "new music" was not just a vanity project, an easy way to stand out against the competition. "He didn't mince words," she said. "I think he was afraid that if the organization did anything for me, they'd be criticized for selling out."

But Elana pushed back. She had made a few tapes of her music, and offered to play them for him . . . provided that a few younger members of the group were present. "One thing I've learned," she told me, "was that if you accompany an offer with a demand, people take you more seriously." Already, I could sense how this would likely develop. Elana was lining up allies even before they even knew they would be allies.

So, when she finally got to play her tapes, the reaction was euphoric. The older members had tears in their eyes. The younger ones were singing along and clapping – and demanding that Elana receive a live audition. They arranged to hold it at one of their homes.

Elana came prepared. She introduced her parents, whose imprimatur was crucial. She gave a talk, noting that she had immersed herself in Persian music, and wanted to preserve it. "My objective," she told them, "is to provide the cultural wherewithal for future generations." Translation: she hoped to lead a syncretic movement, combining Persian and classical music, so that young people could welcome tradition into their lives. She presented herself as non-threatening.

Part of being determined is to head off the opposition before it gets organized. She knew there were purists who would never condone tampering with tradition. But might they understand that preserving traditions in amber risked losing them altogether? "I was determined," she told me, "to make them realize that the world was happening all around them, whether they cared to acknowledge it or not."

The live audition came off brilliantly. After drinks, a majority of members decided that the group would sponsor quarterly concerts at a local performance venue. They would be advertised, and open to the public. Elana would be paid her usual fee, assuming the concerts broke even. When the group's leader got up to speak, he observed that he had come to appreciate Elana after having initially been skeptical. "What I liked," he said, "was that you could still hear our music. It's there – just updated." Elana might have been a little more technical in her appraisal, but she was happy. She told me, "It's up to me to make them appreciate what's going on. This is a start."

I thought perhaps that once these concerts commenced, she would stop seeing me. But she didn't. After the first one, she told me "I have an idea. I need to start a chamber group." It would go on tour, and popularize what she now called Persian fusion. What did I think? By way of telling her to go ahead, I said "Why not call it the Persian Cats?"

Elana had found her calling. She would preserve tradition by running it through a kaleidoscope – it would continue to change but still be recognizable. As to the practicalities of starting – that is, leading – a chamber group, she knew the obstacles. She would have to find an orchestrator, and train the musicians. "A lot of serious people are turning towards ethnic traditions. So, they can learn mine." It would be hard work, and a lengthy process. You don't just pick up a new tradition. "Time is always an obstacle," she said, "especially when you need to earn a living. But if I'm determined, they'll get in the spirit."

She was determined to make her group-mates determined.

As of now, she is holding auditions ("a lot harder than mine," she assured me). She spends the rest of her time developing people's ear for Persian musicality, so that they'll be able to riff on it. She's had to read up on the theory, just so that she can teach it. "I don't want people just playing notes," she said. "I want them to think in the idiom." She wants them to understand that they will contribute to the sound. "I'm determined to make this a cohesive group. We'll all contribute."

So, Elana turned assimilation back on itself. She accepted it, but on her terms. She now assimilates Persian and Western culture. She anticipates obstacles, and deals with them. Look at what she has done so far:

- She took one step at a time, consolidating her position before moving to the next, e.g., she did not start her own group until she knew that that she would have an audience
- She found allies within her target constituency, and used them effectively – pushing against cultural norms, but with credible back-up.
- She made cogent arguments that convinced people that change was the only way to conserve tradition – in effect, she supported the prevailing position even as she challenged it (and she struck the right balance).
- She never took the easy way out, and never let her bandmates take it either. She showed people that she was working to gain their trust.

Elena's story is somewhat like Dov's in the previous chapter: both are promoting a type of cultural adaptation from within. Both profoundly understand their constituency, and operate accordingly (incrementally, inoffensively, with a message that appeals to the constituency's desire for self-preservation). To offer change is not inconsistent with presenting oneself as supporting continuity. It requires a maintaining a fine balance. Where Elana differs from Dov, however, is that she leans more towards Burt's entrepreneurial spirit. She has big plans. She's starting something new.

So, ask yourself:

- Once I start bringing about change, do I have the interest, imagination, background, and grit to initiate something sustainable, i.e., to turn it into a career?
- Do I define determination broadly, in the near- and longer term?

Elana could answer both these questions positively. It is what made her a successful leader in a new field of music.

Here, a mid-career guy who thought he had run out of options determines to make a come-back. But how? He draws on his experience and his personal resources, at each stage leveraging what he knows. He pulls himself up by his bootstraps, making the most of his position – wherever that happens to be. He sees the possibilities in every position, even as he understands its current limitations. For him, "determination" becomes an exercise in imagining where his own next steps will lead. He takes charge of his own evolution, never overreaching, always incremental, but always well considered.

The first crucial step in his evolution is to assess what he knows and how he can build on it. He was once a leader, so he must determine how "once" translates into a "now" of radically changed circumstances – he is back in the U.S., having lost his perch in a foreign corporate culture where he was a success. So, what elements of his past success can he draw on? The process of making that determination is slow, and there are detours. But each time he fails, he learns something, incorporating it into what he knows about himself. This effort defines determination for him.

After a while, he discovers core capabilities that allow him to transition from one industry to another, and to discover analogies between those industries that he had not realized might exist. Once he accumulates a critical mass of knowledge – about himself, about the possibilities that he can tap into – he ramps up his efforts. The process is sometimes fitful, even nonproductive. But a pattern of success (of successive successes) emerges. We learn from this story that determination results from positive feedback: emerging self-awareness creates – and benefits from – an ability to seize opportunities as they emerge, while those opportunities lead to enhanced self-awareness. Determined people are energized by determination.

As you read this story, consider these factors:

- *Leadership sometimes requires transition from your comfort zone into a new environment. Is that prospect frightening, or does it excite you?*
- *If it is exciting, are you prepared to draw on what you know and then present it as useful in your new environment, i.e., as important knowledge that a new employer should value?*
- *Are you able to overcome loss of a career by turning mourning into an effort to resuscitate yourself? Nobody wants to take a leap of faith, so have you adequately prepared?*
- *Can you build on one success to generate an even bigger one – for example by continual reinvention of yourself, expanding the cohort of people who will appreciate you?*

All these questions translate into whether you have sufficient determination to recover your moxie when you've been dealt a blow. Determination, in this instance, requires a type of nimble coordination between who you are, whom you have been, and what both say about what you can become. Though we ostensibly live Now, we really inhabit a space filled with past experience, as well as prospects elevated (or sunk) by that experience. The following demonstrates how such coordination is possible, provided you remain attentive to how seamlessly these phases of your life segue into each other.

Finding Your Niche

Leaders Make Their Past Count in the Present

When Rick walked into my office, he felt rudderless. "I'm 40 years old," he said, "and I still haven't figured out where I'm headed." Maybe he was daring me to come up with some idea he hadn't yet tried. "I can't tolerate another false start," he sighed. "I've run out of possibilities."

People who feel exhausted from trying, often try to transfer responsibility for their lives to someone else – one last, desperate Hail Mary pass. But, of course, that's not what I was there for. Rick had to draw on his own resources. So, I threw the pass back and said, "Look, let's figure out what resources you can draw on – starting with yourself." However we contrive to be determined, we never start from zero. We have personal experience that can help us to pick up where we left off. So, if we have ever succeeded at anything, we can do it again, even if we've racked up failures in between. Our experience should provide us the necessary confidence.

Rick's case was ultimately a prime example.

In his twenties and early thirties, Rick had been hugely successful. He'd spent ten years in France developing an educational technology platform that helped companies train personnel. "France was way behind in the field," he told me, "so I had a clear shot. They're instinctively bureaucratic, and I was talking modern management." The company was so innovative that *Le Nouvel Econonomiste* and *Alternatives Economiques* ran stories. *France-Amerique* hailed Rick as a great example of cultural exchange. He was a leader. He had thought of branching out into other Francophone countries . . . until his financial backers sold their share to an international conglomerate that installed its own team.

All at once, Rick had no job.

The conglomerate gave him a decent fee for leaving without a fuss. "But you know," he told me, "the money was irrelevant. I was somebody and then I was nobody." He returned to the U.S. with his family, and wondered what he could do. Since he understood tech (or thought he did), he tried working for a small start-up. But its culture was fiercely competitive, and he quit. "I guess I was accustomed to the Code du Travail," he said, "and couldn't hack our workplace norms. You know, France still has a 35-hour work week." The transition only got worse when he was hired by an established company in a middle-management position. "I guess I still thought of myself as able to run things. I could, but they wouldn't let me." So, he quit again.

But Rick *had* been a leader in an important field, and I was sure that with effort, he could do it again. "You have it in you," I told him. "You just need to apply that experience in the right context." Often, we feel cut off from our best selves – from the sources of our self-confidence and feelings of self-worth – because we are not in a situation that allows us to flourish. The trick, therefore, is to find that situation. When we do, the determination that we need to succeed, and to lead, will come naturally. It will *feel* natural, as neither of Rick's previously failed efforts could ever have.

So, I asked Rick what he would like to do. "At this point, I'm not even sure," he said. "Maybe something in education." Okay, that was a start. He had created an educational platform. His younger son had developmental issues, and Rick had studied the options for kids with special needs. "I actually think that the schools are doing a great job, and that I could bring some high-tech expertise to the effort." Getting closer.

Rick did not want to be a teacher, which he understood might be too restrictive, but he thought that community service might give him space to create opportunities for kids after school. He had worked in a YMCA during college, and knew that they welcomed staff-members' initiative wherever they could find it. "I might have something to offer," he mused.

Indeed. This was Rick's experience talking. So, I encouraged him.

Rick went to the local community center, and pitched the idea of developing a basketball team for kids with special needs. It would get them moving, of course, and give them a sense of accomplishment. But as Rick told me later, it would introduce them to technology, since they could analyze games using video-playback and learn to map out strategies. "I told the center's director that this would help the kids learn hard stuff in a stress-free environment – not like in school, where they knew everyone was watching."

The pitch worked. Rick was now a basketball coach. He was leading a team.

But for someone who once founded a company that changed the direction of a country's corporate culture, this was not *the* leadership position that he wanted. So, I asked him, "What in your experience can you draw on that could kick this position into higher gear? You got famous for training people, so how could you do that again – in basketball, but not just in basketball?" I was asking Rick to make the most of where he was, to figure out how to leverage what he had learned in one context (where he was a leader) so that he could acquire some of that same stature again. We all need confidence to use our imaginations, not least to imagine ourselves as having a larger footprint. From that confidence comes determination. I thought Rick could make that transition.

As we talked, Rick told me that the personnel training platform he had developed was high on intra-office communication. "Those French," he said, "were so hierarchical that people rarely shared ideas except in formal settings. My platform taught them to loosen up – and talk!" This was an important perception, since Rick had noticed how the kids on his basketball team were often inhibited, not volunteering their ideas unless he specifically asked for them. "Maybe they sense they have a disability. But maybe it's just the influence of social media – nobody talks anymore." So, I suggested that effective communication, in whatever setting, may not come naturally . . . and that here was Rick's natural opening.

Calling on all his experience, including that of being an entrepreneur, Rick set up a program to help kids at local schools become more effective communicators. He brought in speech teachers and debate coaches, who were happy to work after-hours for extra pay. The center provided the space, and Rick charged tuition to cover costs and pay him a modest stipend. He even advertised:

> This twelve-week program offers modules for making a presentation, for debating and public speaking, and for team-building and leadership. Think of it as Toastmasters for kids.

In no time, the program was swamped with applicants. Rick set up satellite programs in other local venues, and more teachers and coaches asked to join the faculty. Suddenly, Rick was leading a major initiative, getting kids to be confident on their feet. There were even alternative programs for special needs kids, which his own son wanted to join. Teachers in the kids' regular classes reported that they saw a remarkable improvement in communications skills – as well as in overall confidence.

Rick continued to see me. By the time the pandemic hit, he was managing over 20 venues, and educators from other towns were studying his methods. He was earning a decent salary, and felt that (once again!) he was both innovative and a leader. The pandemic was, of course, a shock to the system and, for 18 months, everything stopped. Rick survived on educational consulting. But now, since schools have reopened, Rick has big ideas. He is taking his initiative public, even thinking of franchising. He has obtained serious financing, and he's involved in branding with a PR firm. "This could be the next Mathnasium – real tutoring for the masses," he told me. "I mean, if kids are afraid of math, they're just as afraid of making a presentation." Right again.

In achieving his current position, Rick did not rely on help from anyone else so much as he drew on personal experience. It gave him the confidence to plow ahead, a sense that his direction was organic to him. For Rick, determination was the natural extension of who he knew he was. Once he got in touch with that, there was no stopping him.

So, here are some ideas to think about:

- To emulate Rick's type of progress, I should search my background to determine what features I can leverage.
- I can develop self-confidence by meeting a need that remains to be met.
- Ultimately, I should not view determination as pure grit, but as some combination of grit, market awareness, and the ability to imagine a future based on what I've already accomplished.
- Accordingly, I should not just mine my resume, but collect market intelligence.
- I should put together a business plan that will attract buyers – or, at least, learn how – and then determine my capacity to pull it off (no business plan is worth much if we cannot find the personal and capital resources to pull it off).

Rick has many traits of a natural entrepreneur – not least, a grasp of what people need and how he can provide it. You do not have to be such a natural, but you do need a good idea of what constitutes a "good idea." The more it is based on concrete experience – which you can rely on, which you can sell – the better. So, sit down and think. Half of pursuing a vision, half of being effectively determined, is just plain mental activity. Then you must get to work.

So far, I have discussed the importance of determination in becoming a leader, but here I emphasize the concomitant idea that flexibility is crucial to determination. Sometimes, we cannot even begin to be determined – that is, determined to lead – unless we can change course and accept a different path for ourselves, even a different definition of who we think we are. In fact, exercising flexibility is especially hard when we are committed to being one version of ourselves while the world around us demands that we be another. If we can't accede to these demands, at least in some ways, we may not become a leader at all.

In this story, a high-powered executive is required to become more congenial/polite/even-tempered if she wants to ascend to the top management post. Initially, she considers such demands a personal affront, and continues to behave as she pleases. But when she finally realizes that her career is at stake, and that change is the only way forward, she sets about learning to be less offensive. She goes on a listening campaign, and demonstrates how (in response) she is willing to change. It's a humbling experience, and she does not necessarily buy in to everything she's learned. However, she appreciates the practicality of conspicuous behavioral change and begins to act accordingly.

This story demonstrates that determination is situational. It takes different forms depending on how much we need to accommodate other people's feelings. We cannot be single-minded in pursuing leadership; we cannot assume that everything is up to us in terms of how well we satisfy objective standards. Subjective standards may be equally important – and much harder to satisfy because they are intangible. We must be willing to learn what these are, and then adopt the necessary flexibility so that people believe that we know how to satisfy them.

As you read this story, ask yourself:

- *Do I resent suggestions that cramp my style? Does any such resentment hamper my workplace relations, and am I able to control it?*
- *Do I see my management style as just fine, so that other people are out-to-lunch when they demand changes?*
- *Am I only capable of personal change amid a crisis where I have no choice? How can I cultivate greater responsiveness, and avoid back-against-the-wall situations?*
- *Am I graceful about changing, or do I display my disapproval, even alienating people who are trying to help?*

No matter how we behave away from work, we must cultivate a "correct" demeanor at work. This is fundamental to being flexible enough to get along with our colleagues, which is fundamental to being a successful manager. When we act out, we should put ourselves in their places – would we like it if someone, no matter how superior their status, presumed to be imperious? Determination is not consistent in showing Who's Boss. Rather, it requires getting where we want to go without losing sufficient support to get there. It means that we may have to cramp our style, even if we don't really mean it. How we really feel and how we act are separate. If we act appropriately, that's enough. After all, you can't go to jail for what you're thinking. (I've pulled that sentiment from Frank Loesser's famous song, "Standing on the Corner," 1956).

So, observe my client Denise as she takes these truisms on board.

Getting Past Your Reluctance

Flexibility Enhances a Leader's Credibility – It Tells People that You Are Determined to Lead

Denise did not come to see me on her own initiative. The HR office at her firm insisted that she seek advice on "interpersonal effectiveness." What that meant, she told me with obvious contempt for the circuitous locution, was "They think I don't play well with others. They want me to learn." But since Denise was 47 years old and a senior partner at an international accounting firm, she really meant to convey how incongruent that directive was relative to her age and status. "They just want everybody to be nice so there's no complaints. HR hates people who leave blood on the floor."

Clearly, Denise felt that anything we could accomplish would only diminish her "effectiveness," and that HR's attempt to alter her hard-edged demeanor was just a ploy to make their jobs easier. "I get things done," she told me. "So, what if I'm not Miss Personality?"

The problem, it seemed, was that Denise had to accept that senior people do not exist in their own bubbles. They're out there, in the world, subject to everybody's rules. They need to inspire loyalty, and be able to call on people further down the chain to make their best efforts. Denise's real challenge, which HR understood, was whether she could summon the will to change her persona – maybe from Dragon Lady to something less menacing. The firm needed Denise, but she needed to change. Did she have the determination to make the transition, to get over her initial reluctance to change? Could she, in other words, summon the will to become an effective leader? Could she exercise sufficient flexibility so that she did not just spin her wheels?

The issue was particularly acute since Denise was under consideration to become the firm's first female CEO. A lot of women at the firm were pulling for her, but they might be reluctant to accept her leadership unless they were sure she would not offend the very people whose help she would need. So, I put the question to her, "Are you willing to get past your reluctance to change – that is, to conform to other people's expectations – in order to be an effective leader?" I realized that Denise's ego was on the line, since she wasn't used to answering to anyone's demands, certainly as regards her behavior.

Recently, she said, she had chewed out a mid-level manager for not packaging some presentation materials in the same order that they appeared in the accompanying video. "I told him that he wasted the client's time, and should be selling empanadas from a cart downstairs. I said if it were up to me, I'd refund the client's retainer from his salary." What struck me, however, was how surprised she had been when the manager complained and HR supported him. "I got this email saying that while the guy's performance had not been perfect, I could have dealt with him 'in a less offensive manner.' They really hated that reference to empanadas, since the guy was Hispanic and we're trying to increase the firm's diversity."

Denise needed sensitivity training on top of lessons in good manners. But I thought it would help her get past her reluctance to change – that is, to face herself and recalibrate her impulses – if she could start acting more acceptably right now, before HR came down on her even harder. "You know," I said, "the firm has given you a pass for a long time, but they won't keep doing it if you want to remain in contention for the leadership. They're finally looking at you critically, and they seem not to like what they see." I may have scared her.

But Denise still offered excuses. She claimed that her conduct towards subordinates displayed Tough Love, like what she received when she was growing up. "My father always said that the only way we shape up is when we're humiliated, and need to do better to avoid further pain." Okay. Maybe that worked in Denise's family. But when your personal experience conflicts with the real-world demands of your current situation, you should apply tough love to yourself. You should get past your reluctance to act in ways that seem unaccustomed – even uncongenial – but that comport with the norms of the world as it is. After all, no matter how important you are, the world is ultimately in charge, not you. If it demands flexibility, then that's what you have to display.

So, I asked Denise, "Why don't you try apologizing to that guy you insulted? It may seem uncomfortable, but it could be a break-out moment – the start of a trajectory towards 'interpersonal effectiveness.'" My theory was that once Denise became more deliberate, more conscious of how she treated people, she would treat them more acceptably. I never expected her to *want* to treat people nicely, but I knew that if she wanted the leadership badly enough, she would make the effort. She had to start practicing self-discipline. She had to mount a *determined* effort that would amount to visible change (even if, deep down, she never acquired the humility that would have made that change a natural part of her personality).

Determination sometimes requires that we act against the grain of our natural inclinations. That makes it harder but, sometimes, even more necessary.

Two weeks later, Denise reported that she had apologized. "He probably wondered if I was sincere, but I promised that I would never insult him personally again. I think it was that promise that mattered." She also wrote to HR, and advised them that she was taking a course at NYU's Stern School of Business on how to conduct difficult conversations. The course was taught by this woman who developed a program for business leaders caught between conflicting demands. How do you know what to say in such instances so that no one is offended? "In my case," she told me, "there are the demands of my real inclinations and those of everyone else. I guess if I want to lead, I should learn to reconcile those demands." By "reconcile" she meant "be flexible."

Denise approached this effort from the perspective of self-interest. Neither she nor I expected that her brain chemistry was about to change. But like everything else that Denise undertook, she was making a commitment to manage the problem that faced her. She was determined to adopt a more conciliatory affect. "I know that everyone thinks that I'm bossy, even bitchy, and I have to start acting differently." What I heard, was that Denise was determined to get past her reluctance to alter her demeanor, that is, her sense of entitlement to any demeanor that she damn well wanted. No one would give her a lie detector test but, if she could control herself effectively, they would welcome the change.

Denise being Denise, however, she did not depend on anecdotal evidence to help her clear the substantial hurdles that HR – and, by implication, her colleagues – had set up. She determined to prove to them, beyond question, that she understood what would be required of her in any leadership position. Accordingly, she used her six weeks of annual leave to take a tour of the firm's offices, both in the U.S. and abroad (she made ten stops in all). In each case, she sat down with executives and, in some cases, mid-level managers, to learn about what they wanted in a leader. Most people, of course, wanted someone who would keep the firm profitable. But she insisted that they also speak about personal qualities. When she returned, she reported to me that almost everyone wanted an empathetic leader who recognized the competitive demands of big-time accounting, and helped everyone perform at their highest level of competence. They wanted someone who was on their side.

"So, you know what?" she said. "I wrote up a report about my tour, and made clear what qualities people want in a leader. I didn't say a word about my ambition, but I didn't have to."

Denise showed extraordinary determination to overcome her reluctance to change. In effect, she advertised it. The arc of her experience demonstrates that determination to lead is based, in part, on confronting oneself and, crucially, getting past a reluctance to change your persona. In a word, it demands flexibility.

Denise is still working on herself. If she does not get the leadership position, will she go back to her old ways in a fit of disappointment? My sense is that she has learned too much to ever go back there again.

We learn certain principles from Denise's experience:

- Sometimes, leadership requires us to work against our inclinations, so that we can meet others' expectations. We should be ready to accept that.
- Flexibility is not just a way to approach business challenges. It is also a necessary factor in solving personal problems that keep us from being effective in business.
- Determination is flexibility is another key insofar as we are required to change (sometimes drastically) to achieve our objectives.

Denise finally accepted that her attitude had to change. A determined leader recognizes that, when the tide turns against them, they must swim in a new direction. Being flexible does not detract from determination – it's part of determination.

Moreover, in becoming flexible, Denise did not do just enough to probably get by. She used real imagination (as in writing that report, demonstrating how leaders ought to behave towards colleagues). It would be absurd to think that she did not intend to live up to standards that she personally, conspicuously announced. So, we learn that flexibility is not just some rote response to demands, but rather an opportunity to show concern and good faith. Denise figured this out because she had to – but she made a determined effort.

The young man in this story also displays the requisite flexibility, but relies as well on another trait that allows him to be flexible: empathy. He works hard to understand what other people need and expect, so that he can negotiate effectively. That is, he realizes that he will not be able to lead – in this case, an experimental music venue – unless he makes the compromises necessary to draw people into his enterprise. He realizes that being a leader is not just about oneself but, rather, about creating a group of people who feel that one's leadership also serves them. The balance is delicate, since there is no value in conceding too much. But without striking the right balance, no deal may be possible at all (i.e., no one will want to be led).

In part, determination is about knowing how to revive an offer in order to get to Yes. It's about the willingness to make concessions – and then make the most of them because you've hired the right people and created a context where they will feel loyal. In fact, flexibility is what lawyers would call a "condition precedent" to loyalty, in that unless you are flexible your troops will feel no inclination to follow your lead. They should believe that you understand their best interests and are taking them into account.

So, flexibility and empathy are two sides of the same coin – certainly in a leadership context and, more generally, as we proceed through life. In the previous story, the hot-shot executive never really felt empathy, and had to make do with learning to act as if she did. Here, however, the young man feels considerable empathy because he and the people he hopes to lead share several common objectives. He determines what these are, and uses them to appeal to the people he hopes to draw into his orbit. It is the foundation of a successful strategy – even though it virtually comes naturally to him, and feels less like a strategy than the way he might naturally do business.

Of course, his modus operandi is immediately plausible because he operates in a familiar space. It may be harder to execute in unfamiliar territory. Then an aggressive learning process may be required. Eventually, however, we can learn enough to develop empathy, which we can deploy as we work to become successful leaders.

As you read, ask yourself:

- *Do I understand the concept of empathy? In practical terms, it means the capacity to imagine what other people feel so that you can respond to their needs.*

- *Am I naturally empathetic, or do I have to work on it, especially in environments unlike the one that I ordinarily inhabit? Am I willing to do the work?*
- *If I display empathy, do I expect a quid pro quo, i.e., something in return? As a natural response, empathy is no transactional. It should not be confused with making a bargain.*
- *Do I display empathy initially and strategically, but then expect people to look out for themselves like "adults"? Half-hearted, grudging empathy is easily detectible, and won't help you in the long run.*

In business settings, it's tempting to dole out empathy as if it were a perk, i.e., some kind of reward. But actually, it is a means through which individuals can effectively relate to each other before ever coming to an agreement about anything. It signals that we take other people seriously, even if they do not share our ideas and objectives – thus making them more likely to respond in kind. Though empathy used to be considered a soft skill, it is now regarded as essential for workforce management. This is because empathy is the basis of trust. No one will trust you if they see no evidence that you understand their point of view. This is why former airline pilots are often chosen to be airline executives when they age out of flying (these guys naturally understand of the stress of being in the cockpit, piloting a plane, dealing with all the technology). So, observe how my client Henry displays empathy, and how his understanding of others gives him the necessary flexibility to lead.

Making the Case

To be Flexible, Leaders Need to Show Empathy for Those They Lead

When Henry walked into my office, he said "You know, I feel like I need a whole consulting firm. I have so many challenges in so many dimensions." Was I supposed to respond in all these "dimensions?" Initially, if only to cover my flank, I observed that "My job is to elicit your own creativity." But then I realized that throwing the ball back to Henry was the right response – not just a facile reflex. Henry was smart. He would figure things out, provided he was assured that he *could* figure them out. "Let's start at the beginning," I said, "and locate the points where you feel stuck. Then we can talk about how you'll work past them."

At the time, it hadn't occurred to me that Henry's difficulties would require an exercise in leadership – or, as it turned out, a type of creative leadership that involved making a case to people who weren't sure they wanted to be led. In Henry's world, everyone was independent, joyously free-spirited, or at least accustomed to keeping their options perpetually open.

But as we spoke, I realized that all these people were not just scenery, i.e., the setting for Henry's personal dilemma. They *were* the dilemma, posing an array of challenges to where Henry felt that he needed to go. So, he would *have* to lead – he'd have no other choice – bringing people out of eccentric orbits into one where he was at the center. It would not be easy.

Henry's world comprised music and musicians, performance venues, recording studios, concert audiences, and intimate audiences. It was a world where each musician and every band felt that their sound was unique. In this world, everyone was demanding, from the hootenanny picker at a one-night gig to the downtown club that booked only stars. Nobody ever compromised, least of all on a sound, since it was always possible that as more people heard a sound it would become the next K-pop. Or Cardi B. Henry called the denizens of his world egoists, prima donnas, and unabashed capitalists – and was gracious enough to include himself.

But he also observed that his environment was not entirely cut-throat. "I don't want to give the wrong impression," he said. "You find a surprising amount of loyalty – which is part of the problem, since nobody switches commitments without good reason." If he invited other people to join his bandwagon, so to speak, he could be seen as disruptive. "I mean," he said "any time you try to make your own way, and other people have to *commit* to you to make that happen, there's always blowback from the crowd that hates The Man and anything too organized."

I was beginning to see that my role would be more than providing encouragement. Henry would need to formulate a sophisticated approach, which challenged an entrenched skepticism but did not seem like a threat.

Henry was a talented pianist and composer, recently out of conservatory in Boston. His teachers hoped he would follow his classical heroes – like Cliburn – onto the concert stage and, for a while, he tried. "But it wasn't me," he said. "I couldn't play my own compositions, and I wanted to be creative – so I stopped touring." Henry wanted me to help him think about how to integrate music into his life on his own terms. "I want to compose and perform and make a living at it. Is that impossible?" I heard frustration in that question, since he'd actually played one of his compositions at the Central Park Bandshell but had received nothing except for expenses. "By the time I paid the back-up trio, I might as well not have performed at all."

So, the question was: how could Henry break into – or, rather, design from scratch – a way of performing his work that could also support him?

Though Henry could play anything on the piano, from Gershwin to Rachmaninoff, he liked to experiment with a 12-tone scale augmented by electronica (that trio in the Bandshell was made up of wizards on multiple synthesizers). He had posted a few performances on YouTube, and even found some kindred spirits. "People want to extend the limits of conventional ensembles, so how do

I draw them into a sustainable audience? How do I get a back-up ensemble that's more reliable than the itinerant hobbyists on Craigslist?"

In other words, Henry wanted advice on how to become his own kind of professional. For that, he would need to lead a movement where like-minded professionals were drawn to him and where, as a group, they could perform beyond the confines of a YouTube channel. Probably, he would need a dedicated venue. So, we set out to discuss his next steps.

We started with the venue, since Henry saw it as a draw. "I'm thinking of a place where other musicians feel comfortable experimenting," he said. "It wouldn't have to be electronica, but that would be part of the mix – performers would come for the synergy." So, Henry envisioned a sort of repertory space, where his own group would be a staple (once he formed it), while other performers would come for the musical excitement while they drew a larger audience.

The challenge was finding a space, then financing it. That meant an initial investment and ongoing maintenance. Henry nosed around downtown. "Downtown," he said, "signifies what's new. It's happening – it's the opposite of David Geffen Hall, and it draws a different crowd." In that spirit, he finally found an old club in a loft where there used to be a button factory.

He approached some event producers with what he thought was an irresistible pitch: if they provided funds to rehab the place, and to keep it running while he built an audience, they could share in the profits for ten years. How could that miss? He expected profits to grow exponentially once people picked up on his vibe.

But the producers were skeptical. They were in business to make money *now* – not in some rose-colored future where people got hooked on experimental sounds. So, we talked about what he could do, and how he could bring them around. "You know," he said, "it's that old problem. No one wants to shake up a system that works for them, even while they claim to be adventurous." So how could he make them more comfortable? How could he sweeten the deal *now*, maybe by front-loading the profits?

Henry thought for a moment, and I think this is where his determination kicked in. What if, he suggested, he could offer them a chance to record some sessions? He wasn't keen on bringing in engineers – and wasn't sure that the other groups would go for it – but if this is what he had to do to get off the ground . . . well, he'd have to convince them too.

When we spoke again the following week, Henry had obtained a commitment from four producers, each of whom would advance funds provided they could record selected sessions over a five-year period. This was in addition to the (eventual) profit-sharing arrangement that Henry had already offered. "They'll lend a certain commerciality to the place," Henry said, "and they'll favor some groups over others. But the venue will be up and running." He hadn't dared to ask for a cut on the downloads. Still, he had managed to corral hard-nosed businessmen into joining up with a performer who had little more than a gleam in his eye.

This showed leadership. Henry had been flexible enough so that his determination did not come off as stubbornness. He had understood what he could concede in order to keep on keeping on towards his goal of a downtown performance venue.

Now he just had to use that same M.O. to build his own group; attract other groups; build an audience; and support himself without running around the country performing one-night stands. "I guess I've learned something," he said. "No one in this business likes to compromise, but if you can appeal to their self-interest it won't feel like compromise."

So, Henry began recruiting back-up players for his group. Since most of these guys viewed themselves as creatives – much as Henry viewed himself – he could not just offer them back-up status. "No one would go for it," he said. "So, I emphasized the improv side of experimentalism – everybody would have a hand in developing the sound." That is, Henry led by appealing to an anti-top-down mentality that favored the group. He knew these guys might not hang around forever (they'd eventually go out on their own) but, at least initially, he'd attract them with the chance to feel like they were living up to their potential. "I was just being shrewd," he said. "I would want the same chance."

More than that, I thought he was being empathetic, whether he knew it or not. You cannot be flexible – or, rather, effectively flexible – unless you appreciate the other person's position, i.e., their goals for themselves in any negotiation. Henry understood how these guys felt, and turned it to his advantage even as he allowed them to feel comfortable in agreeing to join him. He exercised a kind of emotional intelligence which is crucial in business, especially where people's egos and sense of themselves are at stake.

Before Henry went out to recruit other groups, who would play while his own tried out new techniques, we sat down to talk about strategy. "We're all separate, and we all want to be successful," he said, "but there should be a shared purpose. We're all trying to raise awareness of the downtown scene in experimental music." So, I asked him to think about what he could offer these groups so that they would commit to becoming regulars – say, twice a month for the next year or two.

After a couple of weeks, Henry reported that six groups had signed on. "I told them that the risk to any experimental group was that it might become inbred. I offered contiguous rehearsal spaces, where they could sit in on each other and learn how new vibes got real." This was a brilliant move. On the one hand, rehearsals were invariably private – Henry was challenging a norm in an industry where everyone protected their identity. But on the other hand, Henry made people conscious of the risks entailed in adhering to these norms. "It's part of being experimental," he told them. "You have to get past how you've always done things if you want to get somewhere new."

This made sense, at least to groups who already thought along the same lines (just not when it came to rehearsals).

Besides, rehearsal space was at a premium. If Henry could provide space, the groups would not have to scrounge around for on-and-off locations where they could park for a few days, only to be shuffled out when the next tenant arrived. He could save them a ton of time, as well as the costs of packing and unpacking. So, Henry offered the practical along with the aspirational.

Part of the determination/flexibility dyad in becoming a leader is to understand – and then appeal to – how another person thinks. Here, Henry had a built-in advantage since he tended to think just like they did. He just had to instrumentalize what he knew. He had to become conscious of how *he* would react in those people's situations as they sat opposite him, discussing a potential deal. If he hadn't had easy access to this knowledge, he would have had to try harder, putting himself in the other people' places. In any case, he would have had to extend himself and compromise, since leadership involves helping people to understand the merits of sharing of your goals.

Right now, Henry's club has been up and running for a year. However, six months ago he discovered – in addition to whatever money he made – that he'd need another "angle" if he hoped to stay afloat. So, after getting his band to agree, he brought in a twice-weekly DJ whose music (to quote Henry) was somewhat less curated. This was not part of his vision. But as he told me, "I have to live in the real world." The real challenge, however, came from the local board, since DJs bring noisy crowds and (gasp!) dancing. Henry had to convince the board that if crowds came for the dancing, they'd get so hungry that nearby restaurants would benefit. It was a tough sell, but he got a few restaurateur buddies to support him. He succeeded.

So, he's making ends meet. His financing is still intact. Though he was at first skeptical, he's come to like the background recording ("our sound feels so spontaneous"). Now even some DJS want in on the recording deal (with Henry taking a cut as broker). As Henry sees it, leadership means always readjusting to circumstances, never letting up. He told me "You're always making new offers, taking new compromises. You just have to stay one step shy of giving away too much."

I know, it sounds like brinksmanship – or maybe like cocksure bravado. But in a world where you want to stand out amidst competitors with the same idea, it's good advice. So, consider what Henry learned:

- Determination is not always sufficient in dealing with people who have their own interests, and who are invested in their culture. You must show that you understand where they are coming from, and are willing to accommodate them.
- Accommodation can be a win-win proposition, provided you get people to Yes and can still carry on with most of your objective intact.
- People want to be heard. They want to be valued. Leadership consists in showing people that they can express themselves – and be themselves – even in your enterprise.

Many stories in *Everyday Leadership* deal with how potential leaders negotiate a different (religious, ethnic, musical) culture with its own entrenched ideas. In each case, they had to bring these cultures into alignment with their leadership aspirations. They all needed to show flexibility along with determination. Henry understands that flexibility in such instances requires empathy – which in practical terms, requires that he appeal to these others' interests and take steps to address them. As I have emphasized throughout, compromise (usually a clone of flexibility) is crucial, provided that it does not entirely undermine your objectives. When you are starting out, you almost always have to compromise. As you become more established, you may need to compromise less, if only because people trust you more. The point is that when you want to bring people along, and they have strong views, you must appreciate their perspective and show that you respect it.

In this story, a doctor assumes a new leadership position which seems initially daunting. However, she is determined to meet the challenge. What distunguishes her effort is that she doesn't try to do too much too soon. To the extent that she innovates, she is also measured. She knows what her constituency will tolerate – maybe even like. She strikes the right balance.

What's also interesting is that she is dealing with people who are highly invested in their own professional approaches. She has to figure out how to make them all get along, and even come away from their exchanges convinced that they'd learned something. None of this was easy, but she relied on successful models for these types of exchanges. She did not waste her energy on reinventing the wheel.

She also relied on a brain trust so that she wasn't flying blind. Though she respected her own instincts, she understood that a new person in town can benefit from been-there-done-that colleagues. She did not go it alone. In this sense, she exemplifies the modus oerandi that I have been advocating: leaders operate best in cooperative, communal settings. They build their confidence as they go along. Determination is about learning – and listening. It is about self-restraint, and making useful calculations as to what your constiuency actually wants.

This doctor came off as providing an important service, which is what leaders do. So, think about these questions as you read:

- *Am I able to constrain my ambition enough to make only incremental moves, calibrated to what my constituents will tolerate? Can I figure out in what order to introduce new ideas, so that one seems naturally to follow from the next?*
- *Am I a consensus builder, even among a group of prima donnas? Can I find out which moves they may all agree on, so as to forestall opposition and take advantage of the group's energy?*
- *How can I build a group of trusted advisors so that I can limit missteps and not lose credibility, especiall at the outset? Will these people trust me enough to want to wirk with me – even be publically associated with me? How can I convince them to trust me?*

Group dynamics are always tricky. You are dealing with potentially balky individuals as well as with their combined strength. It's easy to get hung up, especially when many of those people know each other, may have formed cliques, and really like things just the way they are. In such instances, a new leader has to pursue her vision slowly, and register how each incremental change goes *down with the group's establishment (that is, with those who exercise power within the group). You must temper your own assertiveness. While some new leaders feel that coming on strong right way will show that they're the Boss, this approach often backfires – especially among high-performing professionals who do not like their views to be questioned. So, here is how my client, Dr. Carroll, negotiates these considerations.*

Breaking Patterns, Defying Expectations

Leaders Make Change Incrementally, Based on what Their Constituency Can Tolerate

Even if you have never seen a psychiatrist, you probably think you know what they do. Psychiatrists inhabit popular culture, and hector protagonists in films like *The Prince of Tides* (1999), *One Flew Over the Cuckoo's Nest* (1975), and *Good Will Hunting* (1975). Every Woody Allen movie, it seems, features Woody on a psychiatrist's couch. Police procedurals feel like a piece is missing until dueling psychiatrists descend on the courtroom. Psychiatrists are on call at universities, tech start-ups, and high-end dating services. You might ask, can we ever escape their interventions?

Yet for all their looming presence, psychiatrists are an elusive, somewhat splintered cohort. They are not like, say, rheumatologists or nephrologists, who all practice medicine much like their peers do. Psychiatrists fall into different "schools," and you don't *really* know how they define themselves without digging into their background. For example, there are psychoanalysts (often caricatured) – descendants of Freud who have patients lie down and free-associate four or five times a week. Is this science? Its models of the mind – conscious/preconscious/unconscious (structural) and id/ego/superego (topographical) – were dreamed up by a bearded white guy at the end of the 19th century.

There are several other ways of doing psychotherapy: maybe you're a psychodynamic psychiatrist; or you practice cognitive-behavioral therapy; dialectic behavioral therapy; logo therapy. Some treatments are complementary to psychotherapy like psychopharmacology or resilience training. Neo-Freudians emphasize social and cultural factors in personality development.

You get the point.

So, what do any of these schools have in common, apart from trying to help people improve their mental health? For my client, Dr. Carroll, the question was more than philosophical. Dr. Carroll was asked to direct a prestigious series of psychiatric conferences where, somehow, practitioners from all the different schools would be expected to make presentations and comment on each other's work. Would they be able to have productive conversations, or would they lapse back into vindicating their individual approaches? Could she design the series to ensure that everyone came away feeling they had learned something (as opposed to feeling that they had just endured a chess match with life-size pieces?).

She was about to find out.

Dr. Carroll had been asked to take over as director by her long-time predecessor, Dr. Prince. He'd founded the series 15 years before, and had put his stamp on it. He was an old-school Freudian, known for his adherence to the Master's teachings. But he recognized that times had changed, and that maintaining the series' Freudian demeanor was by now a lost cause. He didn't want his institution to blame him for dropping the ball. "So, at the handover," Dr. Carroll told me, "he said 'it's time for new blood. I think you can give the series a new outlook.'"

Dr. Carrol had started as a pupil of Dr. Prince, but had steadily moved towards psychodynamic practice. She was also on the faculty at a major teaching hospital. Among academic psychiatrists, she was known and respected. Still, she worried whether she could step into Dr. Prince's shoes – and then change everything. "Well," I said, "he must have confidence in you or he wouldn't have asked you." She told me that, probably, he was less impressed by her work than by how she could meet a challenge. "It wasn't easy transitioning from a strictly Freudian to a more broadly psychodynamic practice. I had to learn a lot about different psychodynamic approaches, as well as complementary techniques. There were hiccups."

Her comment explained a lot. So, I suggested that she apply that same determination to organizing the first of the series' conferences. "After all," I said, "you stayed on good terms with Dr. Prince, so you must be able to talk across different schools of thought. Maybe you could design a program where people share their insights – rather than just talk right past each other."

Often, moving ahead is easier when people have "skin the game," i.e., when they have a stake in a positive outcome, and are not just fighting rear-guard actions to defend their turf.

Dr. Carroll thought about that. She observed that a lot of conferences present a case study, which practitioners comment on from different perspectives. "I could do that," she said. "They'd all learn something – potentially, anyway, if they have an open mind." But what I heard behind her suggestion was a willingness to look around, and adapt whatever she thought would work. Sometimes, determination requires that we use what has succeeded already, so we can save our energies for more difficult challenges. Dr. Carroll was not inclined to reinvent the wheel during her first outing. She resisted the temptation to be flamboyant (many first-timers want to make a splash, and declare their arrival at once). She also understood the importance of creating a comfortable environment. "If people like what I'm doing, they'll come back." Smart.

In this regard, she wanted to expand the conference's diversity: more women and people of color. "I'm being 'flexible' with the Old Boys Network," she said. Apparently, she wasn't frightened of being thought political, since all her invitees took an array of positions that people would find *interesting*. "I'm going for quality," she told me. "Quality trumps any appearance of favoring one group or another." She was a skilled tactician, making changes that no one could fault without seeming stuck in a rut. She wanted to make changes that would move the conference in a new direction without compromising its value to the community.

"I actually asked people about whom to invite," she told me. She created an *ad hoc* team of advisors. "I rely on my instincts," she said, "but I like to verify what they tell me." That morphed into an Organizing Committee for the meeting that drew from different institutes and journals, reflecting various schools of thought. She was a lesson in humility, even as she put her own stamp on the conference.

She handled the finances with equal aplomb. "I know everyone likes to be up close and personal," she told me. "But they'll understand if I make some modifications." So, instead of mailing brochures individually to potential attendees, she asked the conference organizer to email the brochures – at considerable savings. Likewise, while she still flew in the Keynote Speaker, she found local talent for the discussants. She persuaded her department chair to waive the cost of the auditorium. Thus, she could invite residents and fellows to attend for no charge ("they're future paying attendees," she said).

Dr. Carroll also wanted to expand the conference's general audience. This was in pre-pandemic days when hybrid meetings with a virtual component were still novel. She arranged through various professional mental health institutes and societies to allow their faculty to attend the meeting virtually. "I can even arrange for them to ask questions and make comments, she told me." People from everywhere could participate. "If they feel they're losing some sense of intimacy," she said, "they'll be gaining a broader access."

Dr. Carroll knew what compromises she could make. If she set up the conference as a learning experience, then wouldn't people want to learn as much as possible? Here was a way for her to present the opportunity so that they (probably) wouldn't complain. After all, they would have a professionally enriching and collegial experience while saving money.

Dr. Carroll was determined to make her version of the conference work. Sometimes, determination requires renovation, even as we try to make people comfortable with the changes. It requires a certain balance. "Okay," she told me. "I'm breaking a bit with the old, while respecting continuity and tradition. People expect change, but also value what's worked and is familiar." She said she would just have to present it so that it both would be in balance.

Apparently, she excelled at creating "balance." She understood her constituents, which is a prerequisite for leading *and* for change. She presented things as new but also calculated to make things work better in the long run. "I'm waiting for feedback," she told me initially, which is just what a new leader should do.

Weeks later, she told me that the feedback had been overwhelmingly positive. So, let's think about what Dr. Carroll learned:

- A determined leader presents change such that it seems advantageous.
- She create a balance between old ways of doing things and newer aproaches, so that no one get rattled by sudden departures from accepted – comfortable – norms.
- She does not seek to reinvent the wheel, but incorporates past practices into her new, updated approach.
- She allows people time to appreciate her new ideas before moving on to the next one.
- She learns who, within a group, she can rely on.

Dr. Carroll understood that changing an institution requires tact, but also a type of creativity that appeals to what people need and don't even know that they need. She does her homework, figuring out what will fly with this group (e.g., they like saving money). Then she advances incrementally. The determined leader understands her constituents' psychology (which, after all, is what she was trained to do). This is not the same as empathy, but it's close enough, in that both require that you anticipate how people will react to one or another actions on your part. Determined leadership – i.e., the wll to get where you want to go – requires a degree of psychologicl competence focused on what other people expect as their due.

***

The stories in this chapter demonstrate that determination is more than exerting your will. It requires strategic thinking and empathy. It requires flexibility, when necessary, but not so much that you just go with the flow. In this sense, determination is a balancing act, where you try to stay on course – neither stumbling nor getting distracted – so that you can arrive at some acceptable version of your original goal. Leaders are therefore tacticians. They understand, sometimes through trial and error, how to make the most of their circumstances at any time. They also understand how to enable people to believe that whatever interests are at stake in a shared enterprise. Henry was great at engaging the people around him.

Frequently, we face obstacles, both to becoming a leader and in seeking to maintain our position. It is important to understand why these obstacles exist – are they external (like reluctant funders) or do they reflect our own prior failures, fears, or hang-ups? Leaders need to analyze the totality of a situation, and then calmly proceed to address the obstacles in their way. Honesty with oneself is crucial if, for no other reason, dishonesty just wastes time whereas candor allows us to see a problem clearly and get down to work. "Work" is key to determination, since leadership rarely gets easier (life is too changeable). But as these stories show, it is possible to define determination broadly, based on how we deploy practicable means to reach ends that may keep shifting but remain in sight.

Here are some of the take-aways of this chapter:

- The determined leader works within the norms of a culture, rather than seeming to oppose them.
- Determination requires flexibility, which requires empathy.
- You are no less a determined leader if you introduce change incrementally – leaders can start small, continuing to build as they (and their objectives) gain credibility.
- The dynamics of any group is a serious area of study, which a leader must understand in order to negotiate their way to credibility – leaders are group psychologists.
- Keep looking around, since there is change that you initiate and change that happens outside your control – in the latter case, you should be ready to respond.
- Leadership is a balancing act between what you want and what may be possible – the best leaders are ultimately able to tilt the balance in their favor (but it's still a balance).
- Gaining influential allies is crucial to leading a group with its own, distinctive culture.

This chapter demonstrates that determination and flexibility are largely inseparable. A leader cannot be so determined that they fail to recognize how others will respond to their initiatives. They need to project concern for others' interests before plowing ahead. This requires self-consciousness as well as consciousness of those affected. This takes work. But that's what determination is.

Chapter III

Planning and Organization

Even though a leader possesses a motivating vision and pursues it with determination, if he or she fails at planning and organization the whole project will likely fall apart. So, it is important to understand what "planning" and "organization" require. When we plan, we look ahead to specific steps that we'll need to take in order to make progress. Organization, however, is less forward-looking than it is concerned with Now – how do I execute the plans that I have put in place, i.e., how do I translate my overall design into the day-to-day nitty-gritty demands of a project that's subject to real people's whims and to contingencies that can gum up the works? Planning and organization are thus two sides of the same coin: you can't have one without the other, and neither one is sufficient on its own. You must specify how you want to get from A to B . . . to wherever you want to end up, and then follow through by taking real-time, effective actions.

So, planning-and-organization, as an inseparable duo, raises a series of questions to consider as you embark on a leadership project. To begin with, the concept largely concerns logistics. In this sense, it's the counterpart to what is discussed in Chapter Two ("Determination"), extending it into day-to-day particulars that delight MBAs but drive the poets crazy. Thus, if we like to think grand thoughts, how do we develop competence in the nitty-gritty? How (conversely) do we keep the big picture in focus when we are mired in the quotidian? Can we know what's coming next, and when to emphasize what? How do we determine the right way to follow through when our plans may be subject to change? Planning and organization are as much a source of anxiety as pursuing a vision; in fact, they're just rubber-meets-the-road versions of that pursuit. Moreover, as in every stage of everyday leadership, we must deal with issues of compromise. How can we rely on others to take the organizational reins (or, at least, share the work) without surrendering (some or all of) our initial vision? This becomes a particular challenge as our enterprise grows and matures.

The stories in this chapter take on these and related questions. They examine organization and planning holistically – both are always in play – even while one, at times, may take precedence over the other. In the first story, a woman takes on the challenge of leading a project that, for her, represents a leap into

DOI: 10.4324/9781003437635-4

the unknown. How do you make plans when you're just getting to know the terrain, when you experience may provide some but not the definitive guide? She learns as she goes along, never getting too far ahead of herself and adjusting her plans to address inevitable contingencies. In the next story, a mature business leader faces the dilemmas entailed in long-term planning. Can you even make plans when the situation is fluid, unpredictable . . . and subject to a potential cash crunch? He learns how to bring in others for support at crucial junctures. The third story involves a young doctor who seeks to lead a project to guide a new drug through the thicket of FDA rules for its approval. How can he be a "leader" when an entity outside his control prescribes exactly what he should do at every turn? He learns that creativity is called for even in an administrative role, and that successful administration is itself a necessary form of leadership. Finally, in the last story, a young professor sets out to organize a massive conference, leverage one resource to acquire the next. Knowing how to gain access to resources – and make the most of them – is crucial to any leadership project.

So, as you read this chapter, think about some of these concerns:

- Planning and organization are inseparable – you should have big-picture skills even while exercising judgment concerning day-to-day, operational details.
- Just as a vision is subject to change, plans can change as a project develops – so, be ready for contingencies with plans that flexible.
- Never dismiss the need for effective follow-through ("I'll just leave the boring stuff to other people") since, without its adequate execution your whole project can fall behind schedule and even fail.
- Learn how to locate and make optimal use of resources, and how to leverage one resource to access the next.
- If you treat people as "resources," never forget to also treat them as people – people are not fungible, and have their own specific needs.
- You can put your stamp on a project as its leader, even if your leadership is mostly administrative – good administration can be creative.

The people in the following stories apply these principles. They learn as they proceed and remain flexible. Plans are not straitjackets. Your organization can change as your plans develop, and as new needs arise. The point is to stay focused so that you can respond in real time with your utmost energy and creativity. Commitment, while crucial, does not mean that you should feel tied down to a particular way of doing anything. To be creative is to be nimble.

This story concerns how to plan when you assume the leadership of a new project. Even if you are an experienced leader, and have developed some leadership skills, you still should plan for a new project from the ground up. There will always be contingencies that you cannot anticipate. Here, a producer of documentaries decides to take on Broadway. She thinks she can do it, but still lacks all the confidence she will need. Precise planning helps to build that confidence. It plays a psychological as well as a practical role as she pursues the project. It enables her to get in touch with the demands of the project, including those it will make on her.

So, as you read this story, ask yourself:

- *Am I willing to acknowledge that my background as a leader may not suffice when I seek to lead a new, different sort of project?*
- *Am I good at contingency planning – that is, am I willing to put aside any conviction that my plans are water-tight and will hold up even during rough sailing?*
- *Do I leave the details to others, or do I get down into the weeds because I know that details can be important to the success of the broad outline?*
- *Do I stay on top of things, and realize when a plan is not working?*
- *Do I view detailed plans as a straitjacket ("I can wing it!") or do I use plans to avoid last-minute, crisis-related scrambling?*

Leading and planning are two sides of the same coin. In a new project, this is even more the case. So, test yourself against Samantha who, in this story, plans her way towards a new venture that, currently, is on track to becoming a success.

Leading a New Project

You May not Be New to Leadership, but Leading a New Project Still Requires Planning

In a game attempt to clarify the role of her production company in the media landscape, Samantha would describe it as "niche." It was small. You never saw its trucks blocking side-streets while actors acted out scenes headed for the Big Screen. At best, maybe the littler screens of art houses. Outside her family, few people knew the company's name – a variation on Surprising Humanity. The idea was double-edged: humanity *is* surprising, but the company also surprises humanity by presenting offbeat stories. The name was clever, people noticed. But more importantly, Samantha felt she was addressing a need. "I present overlooked stories," she told me. "That should move the needle of human progress."

Samantha focused on girls – how they coped with challenges like being adopted, being biracial, finding a sport or, more generally, just growing up. Her stories were intimate, closely observed, but still worldly. They featured the voices of girls themselves, wherever they lived, with subtitles when necessary. "I kept the focus on my subjects," Samantha told me. "I didn't want to intrude." What she did want was to show girls excelling, for example, during Carnival in Haiti when, to everyone's surprise, girls were equal to boys in mask-making ability. "I guess it's been a calling," she told me. "I never did it for the money."

The formula seemed inexhaustible. Over the past few years, Amanda had made several documentaries, as well as fundraising films for national charities (there are dozens of NGOs devoted to girls). Some of her work had even been recognized at Sundance, and had been picked up for streaming by Amazon. The projects were always novel, and they allowed her to display an array of talents. "I write the scripts," she told me, "and I've learned how to license music. I can even scout locations." As an outgrowth of her work, she had also produced some theater – in one case, a play by an author charmed by her documentaries.

So, what was the problem?

By the time she came to see me, perhaps two years ago, Samantha felt it was time to "expand," to climb out of her niche and do something affecting the broader society. She was 40, her kids were in boarding school and, for a self-styled Creative, her life seemed too settled and her work too circumscribed. "I kept doing what I was good at," she told me, "and then soon it was all I did." In addition, her work was self-financed. Even with streaming, the documentaries barely turned a profit, and the NGOs barely covered her expenses.

"I'm always complaining to my husband," she said, "and he's getting sick of me. "'Look, I can absorb the costs'" he tells me, "'so what else do you need?'" What she needed, it turned out, was to lead a creative initiative that she devised, organized, and saw through to success. She needed to face down a challenge, much like the girls whose stories had apparently got into her blood. "I need to mount a Broadway show," she said, catching her breath and watching my face. "I know it's a leap – in scale, in terms of what I know I can do – but it's time for me to try." I never discourage clients, but help them focus their aspirations towards realistic goals. Was Samantha being realistic?

Apparently, Samantha's urge to propel herself towards Broadway had been brewing for some time, spurred by the conviction that Broadway itself now ached for upheaval. "The American musical has run out of ideas," she told me. "I mean, after *The Book of Mormon*, what's really shattered people's complacency? Even *Hamilton* is a feel-good story – okay, the music and lyrics are great." She'd had enough of feel-good offerings. "My instinct tells me," she said, "that musicals can get people thinking again – not just buying the cast album." She would introduce Broadway to the life of a 16th-century martyr, Giordan Bruno, who was burned at the stake as a heretic but who belatedly attained the stature of Galileo.

Where had this notion come from? Was it an inspiration, or a fantasy designed to get her as far as possible from making documentaries? Apart from whether anyone would see a musical about an old heretic, would anyone finance it? Most immediately, did Amanda have the expertise to mount a credible attempt? I always encourage clients to extend their reach . . . but this possibility seemed cosmically distant.

But of course, I didn't want to let my skepticism inflect Samantha's thinking. So, I started with Bruno (by way of easing into her own motivations). "What do you actually know about him?" I asked. "Does his life translate into two hours of song and dance?" Little did I know!

Bruno was an Italian philosopher, poet, cosmologist, mnemologist (memory expert), and Hermetic occultist. His cosmological theories extended to include the then-novel Copernican model (abhorred by the Church). Though he began as a Dominican friar, he later denied core tenets of Catholic doctrine, including eternal damnation, the Trinity, the divinity of Christ, the virginity of Mary, and transubstantiation during the Mass. He wandered around Europe until the Inquisition imprisoned, tried, and executed him. Ultimately, he was celebrated as a martyr to science, and is the subject of major modern biographies (as well as turning up in poetry, music, fiction, art, and serious scholarship in multiple languages). A statue to him in Rome stares down the Vatican. Much of his vast oeuvre is (still!) in print, and Samantha had read whatever she could. "I even made a pilgrimage to the site where he was burned," she told me. "His life is recognized as beyond dramatic."

I had to concede that my interest was piqued. We spoke about eternal issues of entrenched authority, and how individuals can be crushed for affronting it. We spoke about genius, and the sometime seamless connection between poetry, mysticism, and science. "After all," she said, "Einstein had a mystical streak. The two are not opposed." But what finally grabbed me, was Samantha's conviction that this man of God could – within the space of a lifetime – come to question everything he had been taught to believe was unquestionable. It was the inner drama of this late Medieval life that, I thought, she would bring to the stage. I imagined a script and a libretto resonating with issues that we still face. If it's not cosmology, then it's transgender rights, access to books, even the rights of girls. "Okay," I said, "I'm hooked."

But then came the real challenge. Samantha had never mounted a Broadway musical – even the plays she'd produced hadn't come close in cost and complexity. She acknowledged being scared, even though she was determined. "At least my family is behind me," she said, "but I know that's just the first step." *Bruno* represented a huge leap into novelty, a total change in long-standing direction. It was as if the trajectory she had been on – small documentaries with minimal financial reward – would now pitch into reverse, with big-time production demands, a big investment, and a possible financial payoff if the work was a success. She would have to make sure that the risk/reward ratio ultimately tipped in her favor.

She would be heading a multi-pronged enterprise that would include writers, researchers, singers, costumers, dancers, financiers, actors, location managers, publicists . . . just look at the credits in *Playbill* the next time you attend a musical. She would have to share control, at least over some aspects of the production. Could she handle the practical, even emotional aspects of what she'd need to do? Could she *anticipate* some of it, to minimize stress down the road? While leadership often entails stress, any stress increases when you take a leap of faith (perhaps an ironic term, given Bruno's apostasy). She had to approach the effort with logic and sufficient self-care.

As we spoke, I advised her that the best way to assume a leadership position of a new enterprise is to have a solid plan. Be as organized as possible.

Contingencies will always arise, but you should leave as little to chance as possible – even while the project takes shape over an extended period. So, we set out to devise a plan that was forward-looking, which over the next year or so would be augmented by careful, studied organization. I was sure that good planning would bolster her self-confidence.

Of course, *Bruno* did not exist. It was an idea, a hypothesis. How would she bring it to life? First, we discussed getting something down on paper, sort of a rough draft of a script (or "book," in theater parlance) that she could show to possible financial backers. But that itself would require initial funding. So, I suggested that she talk with some (moneyed) friends and associates, and interest them in the idea – ideally, winning them over, as she had done with me. We practiced her elevator pitch.

It worked. She obtained enough funding for a researcher/writer to draft a book, delineating the main characters (Bruno, the ecclesiastical hierarchy, his supporters and detractors). She'd have to find an historically-minded writer, but she had some ideas and we discussed those as well.

Once she obtained a barebones book that she liked, she would go back to those potential backers – as well as others – and secure greater funding, enabling her to firm up the book and hold an initial reading with a few potential actors. If all went well, she would secure more substantial funding, based on a budget that would carry her through tryouts in Boston and New Haven before finding a performance venue in New York. Of course, along the way, she would have to locate the out-of-town venues, but she knew that these came up pretty often. She'd need to find audition and rehearsal space. Then, she'd make sure that her permanent investors were still on board (and anticipating Broadway-size profits). She would need to consult theatrical lawyers, and get contracts for everyone. She would have to get a team of writers to refine the book; a group of professional actors; a librettist; a choreographer; stage managers. She would need a set designer, a lighting designer, a costumer. There would even be a platoon of understudies.

Whew! Could she do it all? She felt that she could. To buck up her courage, she would hire a publicist once the show got to its out-of-town venues. "I want to create a buzz," she told me. "It will make me believe in myself." Samantha recognized, apparently, that her practical preparations were an element of her mental, psychological preparation. A leader – especially of a new project – should create their own support mechanisms, since everyone else may be too distracted or just too uninformed to provide the specific support that may be needed as challenges arise.

Even though Samantha had led other projects, she did not overestimate her transferrable skills. Rather, she realized that with sufficient planning and organization she could identify her deficits and address them. "*Bruno* is a kaleidoscope of moving parts," she told me. "I'll get them moving in sync – eventually." She'd have to take the right steps in the right order at the right time to achieve positive, reinforcing results. She would need back-up plans as, for example, if her initial pitch to investors fell flat and threatened the entire project. I told her that, from my own experience, I knew that plans may give way to other plans – the idea was always to be ready. Planning is a form of precise anticipation, not some immovable, blunt projection. All her plans (for writers, dancers, venues, designers) had potential variations, which she could draw on to prevent a cascade of failures. Just as she hoped one good result would make way for another, she knew that the process could play out in reverse – and she made plans to keep that from happening.

In a new venture, where you don't know what you don't know, leadership entails contingency planning, so that surprise is held to a minimum. So, in a perverse way, all this planning is a type a freedom (not a straitjacket) since you won't have to resort to last-minute fixes that may disrupt your other plans and *really* restrict you. You're free to pursue the venture how you set out to.

So, as Samantha began to take the reins of *Bruno*, she focused on some important ideas:

- Even if you have leadership experience, planning for a new venture should be careful and precise.
- Every plan should entail a contingency plan, so you're not caught up short by surprises.
- Planning is a great way to bolster your confidence, since it literally lays out the steps towards where you intend to go.
- Complexity should not be a deterrent, but only a rationale to plan ahead.

Currently, Samantha is refining the book, and making sure that the writers, lyricists, and librettists are working in sync. She meets with them weekly, and listens. The meetings are part of her plan, since she has an idea about how a 16th-century cosmologist-mystic should sound to 21st-century ears – and appeal to 21st-century hearts. "His sensibility has to be prescient," she told me, "even though he is hardly modern." I'm impressed.

This story concerns the vagaries of long-term planning. What may seem like a "plan" can, over time, become subject to multiple contingencies. It can assume a non-linearity that's vastly dissimilar to what you first imagined. In fact, the longer the term, the more likely that contingencies will emerge. How do you deal with them so that you can keep going?

As you read this story, ask yourself these questions:

- *Am I able to lead a project in an uncertain environment where it is necessary to think on my feet and adapt to changed circumstances?*
- *Do I know how to balance quick rewards with long-term goals, so that I can keep my eye on my main objectives?*
- *Can I build a team that will further my plans even as uncertainty continues to affect those plans?*
- *How well do I handle stress, and can I step back when I must make changes to protect my mental health?*

In this story, my client faces these questions, and learns how to address them. He learns that long-term planning is an evolving process, and that he needs to evolve alongside it. Adaptability is a form of resilience which, in turn, allows us to navigate in challenging, non-linear environments.

Long-Term Leadership is an Evolutionary Process

Unless You Can Adapt, You Cannot Lead over the Long Term

George did not look like anyone's idea of some A.I. geek, bent on turning machines into mind-readers. Rather, he looked like what (in one sense) he was: a 50ish businessman with typical, Chamber of Commerce aspirations. His company made digital billboards that, he hoped, would "inform" as many drivers, cyclists, and pedestrians as possible. But . . . these billboards did read people's minds – virtually – as digitally master-minded messages changed in relation to the traffic beneath them. They relied on A.I.-generated logarithms that profiled these people from hour-to-hour. So, while one message might flash in the morning when everyone was focused on work, another would greet them at noon when the streets were full of shoppers. In the evening, when people were tired, the messages were calming. A billboard, which always sold the same product, adjusted its pitch for maximum impact. According to George's data, people felt that the signs were uncannily responsive (he called them "smart billboards"). Such integration of messaging and data set George's company apart.

George had founded the company, Digital Roadshow (DR), about 15 years ago, when he caught himself ignoring outdoor ads. "I knew enough psychology," he told me, "to realize that we get conditioned to seeing the same thing over and over. The mind only reacts to surprise." So, he set out to surprise people by programming billboards to display nuanced messages throughout the day. Once A.I. came along, he attempted another new departure, deploying Big Data to vary his messaging. DR's billboards literally took on a life of their own, seeming to know who was viewing them, and when. Between, say, 3 and 4 p.m. (when mothers were driving kids home from school), the messages emphasized a product's health-and-wellness features, while during the same time on weekends (with cocktail hour in view) messages emphasized the product's easygoing side.

Because DR monitored local CCTV feeds, its data reflected where people shopped – its billboards, accordingly, assuaged their guilt if they might have spent too much. On the other hand, if they had only window-shopped, the billboards urged them to spend with abandon. In every case, the client's product was positioned as a necessary purchase. No wonder his clients loved it.

When George came to see me a few years ago, he knew he'd achieved proof-of-concept results. "Companies who stuck with me had record sales," he said. "DR should set the standard for outdoor advertising." Okay, so what was the problem?

George felt that no matter how much success he had, it was tiny compared to the $8 billion/yr spent on billboards in the U.S. "DR could lead a revolution away from ineffective, static signage to A.I.-powered, dynamic billboards that grab your attention because you don't get conditioned to the message." He felt ready. His algorithm was patented. He had buy-ins from major retailers. He could even claim that DR billboards were environmentally friendly because they didn't have to be put up and torn down every month so that – for a while, anyway – people might notice them. What he needed, he told me, was market access. There was the rub.

The market for billboards is largely saturated. Few highway authorities or city governments will grant permits for *more* billboards, and existing billboards are subject to long-term easements. "No official will risk a public backlash by allowing someone to come in and add to the clutter," he said. "Even if they did risk it, the outdoor advertising lobby would mount a campaign at the highest levels to block the decision." Of course, the environmental lobby would sue. So, DR's billboards were in suburban areas that had recently acquired high-tech campuses, leading to increased road traffic, new subdivisions, and more shoppers at the surrounding malls. Local governments were eager to support any commerce, and the pace of growth was so intense that environmentalists focused on stopping the sprawl rather than preventing a few outdoor signs. DR's market, it seemed, might be limited to such new, middle-class suburbs – bypassing core cities and their connecting arteries, where traffic would always be significantly higher.

So, George asked me whether I thought he could break out of this pattern. "It may be hard to replace the entrenched advertisers," he told me, "but what about urban areas that aren't saturated? What about going international?"

Sometimes, clients pose questions that put me on the spot. I may not have sufficient data to answer their questions. But fortunately, in this case I didn't have to. George's question was rhetorical. He wanted my support for a plan that he was hatching. Basically, he wanted my help in developing the plan, and in figuring out how to carry it out.

George outlined a massive project to place billboards on roadways across LA, and in local Metro Rail stations where advertising was not yet allowed. LA is 502 sq. miles, 60% bigger than New York. The prospect was eye-popping.

"I'm still in the early stages," he told me. "I've spoken with the mayor and some city planners. But the mayor is up for re-election, and the environmentalists will be opposed." There would have to be some well-directed lobbying, even before all the paperwork and likely litigation.

"This could take several years," I told him, "even assuming that circumstances don't change – which they always do." George needed a *long-term* plan, as well as sufficient organization to see it through. For starters, he needed local legal counsel, since even one dissonant move could give ammunition to the opposition. It could scare off people who might, otherwise, provide support.

So, I suggested that we draw up a plan. "A plan is an investment," I said. "If it works, you can adapt it to other projects." At the back of my mind, I thought that *if* George could scale the obstacles presented by LA, then maybe other cities – other countries – would not seem impossible.

George gave himself two years. "First," he said, "I need to hire lobbyists to present the deal to the district boards. Then it will need to be approved by the City Council, and *then* the mayor will sign off."

"But suppose the City Council falls through," I said. "Suppose there is a new mayor, and he's elected with environmentalist support – they'll call in their chits." George thought a moment. A snag? He'd prep his lobbyists for contingencies. "Okay, Contingency Prep," he declared. It's in the plan – and it may take priority as things develop." In long-term plans, the contingency plan may overtake priorities, and I stressed that. Better still, you should anticipate likely contingencies, and build them into the plan using a type of decision-tree model (if-this-then-that).

As we spoke, he mused that he'd have no trouble when it came to selling the ad space. "The billboards will be an anticlimax," he laughed. "It's getting there that's the challenge." I reminded him about hiring a lawyer, and suggested that he budget for legal fees. A budget, in fact, is an initial plan, and accounts for all the major players. "You'll need help supervising so many moving parts," I said, "so put in an item for someone who communicates with the players on a regular basis." He said he would. The plan would be as much about people as about making the right moves. The two are often inseparable. George would keep his eye on the big picture.

The district councils supported the project because it would introduce new income (the Retailers' Association, in collaboration with George's lobbyists, had made that point clear). But at the City level, there were doubters. Resolutions needed a 2/3 majority to pass, and George came up one vote short. At the last minute, one council member changed his mind after telling the lobbyists he was on board. George told me that "An environmentalist apparently texted him during the voting. So, before a definitive count was taken – which we would have lost – we withdrew the proposal." The result was a six-month setback. DR had to regroup, lobby members who might switch their votes in its favor, and then get the proposal on the docket again.

Uh oh, another contingency.

But then just as a majority seemed to re-emerge, the proposal ran into another snag. A local paper denounced "visual pollution," a counterpart of that inhalable pollution (a.k.a. smog) for which LA was famous. George hired local celebrities to dismiss such suggestions. But this incident set him back another few months.

"Do I still have a plan?" he asked me, "or just mounting delays?" I observed that planning demands having confidence in the plan. "You should be willing to accept the planning *process* as non-linear," I said. In fact, the longer the term of the plan, the less linear the process tends to be – or, rather, tends to become, since long-term plans evolve in response to changes in circumstance.

At this stage, George had a sales rep overseeing the lobbyists as well as negotiations with council members. "He's wearing two hats, and spreading himself thin. Besides, he has no background in politics." As we had established at the start of the project, appointing key players was crucial to success. "Maybe you'll need to bring in someone on who knows the ropes," I said. "How about one of the lobbyists?" I thought that if a lobbyist could lobby from the outside, he (or she) could direct other lobbyists from the inside.

A week later, George found a woman who, in addition to lobbying, had a background in PR. "When she's not talking with Council members, she'll have ideas on billboard design." The move raised his confidence (a good hire will do that). The sales rep could go back to full-time selling. George realized that even as he had taken on what he now called his "brave new project," he couldn't neglect DR's ongoing business, i.e., its regular sales out in the suburbs. "I have to keep bringing in money," he said, which is always the case when a new project threatens to overtake a company's core business. "I couldn't do LA if I'm not selling somewhere."

But now I questioned whether the timeline was realistic, even if he maintained current sales. "What if the project takes three years? Or four?" Would the additional effort – and added expense – still be worth it? Overall, did he have the resources to continue that long? On a more personal, psychological level, did he want to keep flying to LA, sometimes two or three times a month, to keep everyone on track? George had three kids, and I could see that he was feeling the strain.

"Maybe I need a full-time project manager," he suggested, "someone to be my eyes and ears, who could report back to me daily."

His plan seemed to evolve even as the endpoint receded. "Can you afford still more staff?" I asked. "I mean, you just hired an in-house lobbyist." Money could be a real issue. But he had the definitive answer: "You know," he said, "when I look at the sunk costs, how can I not afford it?"

There is always an inflection point in every plan, when costs vs. benefits need to be weighed – honestly, irrespective of how "hope" may tip the balance. George understood where he stood, and chose to move ahead. His planning took on questions of his wellbeing. That is, he had to keep himself mentally fit because he was, after all, the pivot around which everyone and everything revolved. So, if his plan now began to take on a certain sprawl, he had made the calculations and knew what he needed.

George told me that for him, "planning" (as well as the follow-through organization) had become an organic process, constantly growing and changing. "If I am directing things," he said, I'm also being directed by how things develop. Maybe that sounds a little Zen, but taking charge means knowing how to respond as things change around you." Clearly, George's idea of leadership had evolved along with the ups and downs of his project. "It's not like I'm letting go," he said. "Far from it! But I'm making the most of where I am at any point, changing course to move ahead." His realization was another version of that non-linearity we had talked about regarding any long-term plan.

As he kept going, there were more snags. George dealt with them. His overall finances had become so leveraged that traditional banks refused to lend him any more capital. He thought he'd have to remortgage his house or sell one of his properties. We spoke about other sources of funding, for example, bringing in investors or reaching out to some friends for a bridge loan. "When I showed them the project," he said, "they believed I could pull it off. But the investors still wanted a super-high return, and my friends wanted 15% interest!" Ultimately, he took on a silent partner with a small stake I the business. "The guy will still let me be the decision-maker – I guess that's comforting."

Yet this "silent" partner had ideas. With connections in Ontario, Canada, he thought there was an opening for DR. That is, with all that George had learned from LA politics, DR could convince the provincial government to let it put up billboards as the road system expanded. "'It's virgin territory,' " he told George, "'and you could show them why they need you.'" It was a thought. It might also be a source of some quick, much-needed income. But the real message was that now, since George had a plan responsive to serial hard knocks, he would be a more agile operator. It was the plan – and its history – that impressed this new guy. George said he'd give the idea some serious thought, provided that this new potential project did not distract him (and his staff) from their work in LA. The partner volunteered to lay some groundwork. It was another development in the planning process which, the partner added, could – in the near term – give a lift to the LA project, not just with cash but with credibility.

So, as a result of this much-extended process, George could claim some important take-aways:

- When long-term plans do not follow their intended course, contingencies will develop that must be addressed.
- The longer the planning process continues, the less linear the plan is likely to become, as each new contingency requires a degree of redirection.
- Budgeting is a form of planning, and the addition of staff – a part of the budgeting process – is itself a form of planning.
- When a plan keeps resorting to "if," it's less a plan than an aspiration.
- Maintaining your mental health – that is, your ability to manage continued stress – must be part of any long-term plan.

Basically, George hung in there. But he learned to adapt, to go with the flow of contingencies that developed. He learned that plans, like the human beings involved in them, are organic, and evolve with time. Long-term plans may look nothing like what they started out as – but that's okay, provided you can follow through with effective organization.

This story concerns a young physician who leads an effort to develop a new anti-depression drug. In view of the FDA's strict system of constraints, he wonders whether he is a "leader" at all – rather than just someone following the rules. Of course, he learns that following-the-rules requires immense organizational dexterity. That is, you must organize effective teams, and orchestrate their effective collaboration. There is plenty of creativity and quick thinking involved.

So, as you read this story, ask yourself these questions:

- *Do I resent rules, and try to cut corners, or can I work within the rules so that, ultimately, they work for me?*
- *Am I willing to accept the idea that organization and administration are still leadership skills, or do I need to set my own rules and operate with unfettered spontaneity?*
- *Can I accept the long view of leadership, or do I need daily confirmation that I am in charge?*
- *Will I spend enough time to understand the system so that I know how to comply and how to recruit others whom I can rely on?*

Leadership comes in many forms, depending on what you are leading. So, learn to adapt. Otherwise, no matter how great your vision and determination, you may not succeed.

Leadership in a Context of Systemic Constraints

Organizational Skill is Crucial to Success when Someone Else Makes the Rules

It's one thing to lead when you can call all the shots ("Follow me! I'm in charge!"), and quite another when you're bound by constraints on what you can do and how you should do it. In that latter case, can you even be said to lead, at least insofar as that term is commonly understood? Worse still, where the government is calling the shots, it can reject what you've done – even stop you from stating over – if you haven't followed the requirements exactly. You may feel like you're trying to lead in a straitjacket. You can't risk being called to account. You stifle any spontaneity. You reason backwards from the requirements, rather than deploying your natural instincts. You resist the urge to shout "I know what I'm doing, so get out of the way!" Even if you're learning as you go along, you apply what you know just to stay within the rules. Finally, if you ever reach your goal, it's because you've learned to navigate the rules, while everyone on your team supports your effort to keep on leading (whatever it means).

My client Michael was in this situation. He was leading the approval process for a new psychotropic drug while contending with the FDA's tangled rules. When we'd meet, he was usually exasperated. "I can't believe what they want," he'd sigh. "And they want it meticulously documented." He felt like the bureaucrats were leading *him*. He'd describe the submissions he had to make, and the back-and-forth that he went through before they could officially be considered submitted. "Everyone I recruit complains that they do things ten times. For a while, we were running out of mice, and then we started running out of human subjects." His point was that it was hard to hold this sprawling project together. When he wanted to cut through the red tape, he'd just encounter more. "I feel like I'm trying to lead from behind," he told me. "Except that from behind, you can't see anything but more government requirements." He felt as though he was burning out. He felt overwhelmed. "Probably," he'd say, "I should never have started this project."

Of course, it wasn't Michael's nature to give up. As Chief Resident in a Clinical Psychiatry program, he was committed to patient care. He had an M.D./Ph.D. with a concentration in psychopharmacology – i.e., he studied the effect of drugs on the brain. So, he "was not starting from scratch," as he'd sometimes say just to reassure himself.

A few years ago, he'd developed a hunch about this drug, and he couldn't rest until he found out if it worked – that is, if it was good enough to be brought to market. His problem was convincing himself that he had the leadership skills necessary to finish the job. He was not even sure what such skills were. "After all," he'd say, "isn't it weird to feel like a leader when someone else is telling you what to do?" His problem was that while he grasped the psychopharmacology, he was unsure if he could leverage that knowledge into a viable, FDA-approved study that would result in a marketable drug.

Michael was struggling with a common dilemma: highly educated people often fret over challenges that require skills that they never studied. "I know what I can do," they'll say – as if that's all they can do.

So, my role was to provide encouragement and, more precisely, to help Michael define his role as a leader within the FDA's rigid system of constraints. I had to help him feel that he was making consequential decisions, and that following FDA protocols (though they were strict) still allowed him to be creative; to exercise foresight; and to manage teams of professionals (not to mention his own capacity to keep on going). After all, he still had to make the *right* choices if he were to follow those protocols. He still had to ensure that everyone communicated, and worked together. "It's how you manage this effort that counts," I said. "Your role as a leader is to ensure that the requirements are met – and that people understand what happens if they're not." In other words, I wanted Michael to appreciate that leading within a system of constraints is just as much of a challenge as when you're making up your own rules. "It's just a different setting," I told him. "But you're no less the leader because of it." Sometimes, thinking inside-the-box is even harder than thinking outside it, since lots of people can dream up new ideas – but how many can do it while conforming to a thicket of rules?

Looked at from another perspective, while the FDA established a general plan (first do this, then do that), it was up to Michael to follow through with good organization (here's the team, here's how to carry out the plan). "So far," I said, "you seem to have an instinct for organization."

Michael needed to hear this. Sometimes I'd repeat it several meetings in a row. It's important to realize what leadership *is* where your work is mostly admin and organization ("I fill out a lot of forms," he'd sigh). Of course, in a context where "leadership" is framed by step-by-step rules, it's hard to see yourself as a leader – rather than as someone who just follows the rules. Your decisions seem to be diminished in scale. But in fact, it's like being a lawyer. The provides the lawyer guidance, but how the lawyer interprets the law makes all the difference to his effectiveness. Okay, so the FDA has protocols, but how you organize your team within them can make you a leader . . . or someone who poorly follows the rules and falls back to square one.

When Michael first came to see me, he had a hunch about ketamine, a compound that seemed to have a remarkable effect on depressive states. When it was used as an anesthetic in surgical procedures, patients reported waking up with a feeling of euphoria. It was also used as a street drug, "Special K" (perhaps, he thought, users were treating depression that they couldn't otherwise get help for). So, Michael wanted to study ketamine for potential use as a psychopharmacologic agent. "If this drug could be adapted," he told me, "with the right dosage and means of delivery, it could be a blockbuster – the next Prozac."

Michael knew it would be an uphill battle, but he couldn't let go of the idea. "I just need to organize the trials," he said, "and then submit the results to the FDA." Little did he realize, at that point, the scope of the project he was taking on. When he had studied pharmacology, he had participated in the development of new drugs, but he had never led the research – he had been off in a corner of the lab, just playing his part.

But now he was *leading* research to develop ketamine as a drug to treat depression. In fact, ketamine *had* been approved by the FDA as an anesthetic, so it wasn't a brand-new molecule. But using it for depression? The FDA would require rigorous trials. It would want to know, for example, the effect of the drug; the dosing; the potential toxicity. How is the drug absorbed, distributed, and metabolized? What is the best route to administer it? What are the side effects, and does race or gender or ethnicity affect its operation? How does it compare to similar drugs in its class, and how does it interact with other drugs? First, there would be test-tube trials, then would come trials on animals. By the time you got to clinical trials on human subjects, the complications increased dramatically: who qualified for the studies, and how many studies do you need? How long should the studies last and, of course, how do the results compare to those in the control groups who were administered placebos?

The whole process seemed mind-bending . . . and this was before the FDA even began its review. If the drug *was* approved and you wanted to market it, there would be more requirements around safety, the potential for abuse, labeling, and directions for use. From end-to-end, the process could take years and billions of dollars. You'd need to start your own company (which meant getting investors) or attract an established company – a Merck, or Johnson & Johnson.

The trick, I told Michael, was organizing a team experienced in the phases of this vast undertaking. He'd need a legal specialist in FDA compliance. He'd need researchers to design and perform animal studies in conformity with FDA protocols. He'd need clinicians to monitor the human subject trials. He'd need biostatisticians. "Team-building is the first job of any leader," I said. "They decide what teams they need and who should be on them." My point was that notwithstanding the FDA diktats, Michael would be exercising recognizable leadership skills by managing the project efficiently and effectively. "You break it down into parts," I said, "and make the parts cohere into more than the sum of the parts." It's what leaders do. It's called organization.

As the animal studies began, I realized that Michael was so close to the project that he might not recognize how well it was going. After all, from day to day you could barely measure changes in the animals' brains. But over the course of the studies, there had been neuronal growth in targeted areas. "A leader has to stand back," I told him, "and take in the big picture. Breakthroughs happen slowly." While Michael was entranced by the idea that discoveries happen in a flash, the FDA assumed just the opposite. You keep meticulous records. The details accumulate slowly. Finally, the picture emerges. "It's like a pointillist painting," I said. "You stand pretty far back, and then stare for a while, before it comes into focus."

This helped. Based on his animal results, Michael summoned the courage to seek an FDA grant to demonstrate ketamine's efficacy in humans. These included people with suicidal ideation, as well as those who had been depressed for years and had not responded to standard treatments. "Now this is a clear instance of good organization," I told him. You knew what would be required, and you figured out how to meet the requirement.

Michael got the grant, and the initial results were impressive. In over 50% of the people who presented to an ER with suicidality, the ideation vanished in a few hours. Sometimes the ideation returned but, in about a third of the patients, the symptoms did not return even over the course of a year. Michael postulated a mechanism of action for the medication like a car that is jumpstarted: once the engine is running again, it just continues to run. He studied the dosing of ketamine in an out-patient setting – the levels, frequency, and means of administration still had to be determined. But, as a sign of the drug's promise, ketamine clinics were springing up in private practices, with psychiatrists and anesthesiologists collaborating to help patients – even before the drug had received formal FDA approval.

I told Michael that one sure sign of leadership is that people volunteer to support you. "All these professionals wouldn't be lining up behind your work if you hadn't demonstrated leadership," I said. "You drew attention to this drug's potential." In effect, Michael had worked the system to his advantage. He *used* the system – the FDA straitjacket – to enlist other people to help push the drug towards approval. He could draw on their results to bolster his own. The point, of course, is that when you're trying to lead within a system of constraints, you can use the system to support your initiative. Michael applied this approach as the process moved ahead. By this point, there was no more talk of "Why did I ever get involved in this?" He was gaining confidence if only because when people seem confident in you, your own self-confidence increases.

But how to deliver ketamine (other than as an anesthetic) was still an issue. If a drug is administered through IV, you need M.D.s and nurses in attendance. This is expensive and – given the masses of people that might be interested – potentially unwieldy. So, was there an alternative? If ketamine were in a pill, then digestive enzymes would break it down and render it inactive. However, Michael's boss, the Dean of the Medical Center and a huge figure in psychiatry, had a novel idea: administer it through the nose. The olfactory nerve is the only cranial nerve with direct access to regions of the brain involved in depression (e.g., the thalamus). Other medications, like steroids, were administered nasally, and clinical trials were underway to administer vaccines that way as well. So, why not develop ketamine as a nasal spray?

Michael told me that he wished he'd thought of that idea. "But," I said, "as a leader, your job is to draw people into the project – and the Dean is a very big draw." Again, he was leading and didn't know it. Because the FDA required that he determine the means of the drug's delivery, he hadn't realized that by involving someone who came up with the idea he *had* been a leader. "In this sense," I said, "the Dean is now a part of your team. You just organized the delivery team."

Moreover, the Dean had the clout to obtain funding for full-scale clinical trials, necessary to bring the drug to market. From idea-man he had transitioned to fundraiser. He could approach Big Pharma. Though ketamine was already out of patent as an anesthetic, it was "novel" (a term of art in patent lingo) as a nasal spray, so pharma companies would be interested in bringing it to market.

Business and academic research often go together because the cost of developing a novel medication can be prohibitive. So, the Dean partnered with a Big Pharma company through a Medical Center office that specialized in commercialization. Ultimately, they developed a ketamine nasal spray, and brought it to market for treating refractory major depression. The Dean was awarded a share of the patent. "But what matters to me," he said, "was that I led this project. I made it happen." In effect he finally recognized that systems of constraint do not preclude your being a leader. Rather, they require that you organize your project to comply with – and make the most of – the rules. We learn from Michael's experience that:

- Organizational skills are crucial to operating within a system that imposes basic rules for success.

- You can turn the system to your advantage by leveraging its requirements, and encouraging people to follow and support you.
- Sometimes, you may not even realize that you're a leader when, in fact, the issue is how to define leadership in context with your project.
- Attentive team-building is central to your success, since you cannot organize everything all at once – organization necessarily requires reliance.

Michael grew in confidence as he began to think about leadership in context with the FDA's requirements. At first, it seemed as though there was no room for maneuver. But then he realized that once you know what maneuvers you'll need, you can organize how to satisfy the requirements – and lead.

The next story concerns a law professor who builds a world-class conference from resources that he had to create. He uses his brains and his imagination to leverage each resource he acquires to help him acquire the next. But he never compromises his principles to acquire them. Instead, he deflects demands for any quid pro quo that he dislikes, offering clever compensations that both parties can live with.

So, as you read this story, ask yourself:

- *Am I good at judging potential resources to leverage on my way to leading a project?*
- *Do I know how to leverage my resources, so that one leads seamlessly to my acquiring the next?*
- *If people are among my resources, do I still treat them as people, or am I at risk of losing them because I lose sight of their own needs?*
- *Am I good at organizing resources so that, together, they are effective – that is, do I see the whole ensemble, however intricate it may be?*
- *Am I able to call on others to help me see the big picture?*

The professor in this story confronts these questions, and deals with them successfully. But he gains insight along the way. As he leverages one resource after another, each incident is also a lesson on what it takes to lead.

Leaders Rely on Resources

The Best Leaders Create Resources – They Use Both Skill and Imagination

Law schools compete (just like lawyers). Every year, they jostle to reach the "Top 20" or even "Top 10," as decided by self-appointed gurus whose criteria they dismiss (but happily applaud when they inch up a notch or two higher). My client Grant, an ambitious young professor at a not-so-top law school, set out to elevate his school's status – and hence his own – by drawing attention to what he called it hidden strengths. "Look," he said, "we have a great intellectual property program (I'm part of it!), but it's under the radar. If I can make those ranking guys take note, then the school wins and my own prestige gets a boost." Maybe he was angling for a salary increase or, down the road, an offer from a higher-ranked school that would never hire from too far down the charts. "My strategy," he declared, "is to get the whole world to notice us. We're that good, so why shouldn't they?"

Okay, if he said so (as a one-man ranking society with his own biases).

But the challenge, of course, was to take a mid-range school that served its local community, and make it *relevant* to IP practitioners no matter where they resided. Sweden? Brazil? Ghana? Check, check, and check. "The fact about IP," he told me, "is that what happens anywhere affects everyone everywhere – there are no borders anymore, since publishing and A.I. and social media are all colliding." As Grant saw it, nobody had to be convinced that IP was of international concern. They just needed a forum to explore it. "People need to learn about new Chinese copyright laws, or a new trademark ruling in the E.U., or whether India will invalidate drug patents. You can't operate unless you're up on this stuff." For Grant, his law school could supply the forum. It could be the place where, every year, practitioners and government officials briefed each other on a year's worth of initiatives. Even better, they could debate each other in a no-holds-barred environment – no press coverage allowed.

Grant could hardly stop talking, perhaps rehearsing his elevator pitch. "Everyone wants to know what's coming," he told me, "as well as what's just happened. They also want to lobby each other, publicly and over cocktails." So, he would develop and lead a conference on patents, trademarks, and copyright from an international perspective. People from everywhere could talk, listen, and make their views known. The heavy-hitters could discuss upcoming litigation, impending rules, and recent significant achievements (for example, how "fair use" in copyright law – a perpetual quagmire – was finally being addressed). While the speakers would be experts, anyone could attend. "We'd rocket up the rankings if we could pull this off," he said.

So, from a leadership perspective, my first question was "How *can* you pull this off – with what? Do you have the financial and intellectual resources to support this project?"

"I'll get them," he said. "I just need to get organized." What he meant, was that he just had to establish his priorities and, systematically, pursue them. So, we spent the next several months developing a comprehensive strategy. For Grant, it's refinement became consuming. I could hear the gears turn every time we met. I realized, quickly enough, never to underestimate someone with the will to find resources – to organize his priorities into a series of reachable objectives – to make his plan a reality. Grant knew what he needed – the trick would be to get it, that is, to be resourceful about acquiring resources. For starters, he'd need to know whom to ask first.

Of course, all big plans initially run through the Dean's office. Grant made an appointment and delivered his elevator pitch.

The Dean was receptive (he was always receptive to whatever raised the school's profile, and attracted donors). But, like deans everywhere, his response was alert to the bottom line: "How will you pay for this? You'll have to bring in speakers from *everywhere*!" But Grant had anticipated just such a response. In the elevator, he had rehearsed another elevator pitch: "I'm scouting resources, and your approval provides leverage. If people know you're on board, they'll support me." In effect, the Dean's support was Grant's first resource. He had surmised – correctly – that the Dean would feel liberated, that is, if he wasn't asked for *money* (but only an imprimatur), he would provide such resources as he had at his disposal (which was what Grant was really looking for). "I can give you the auditorium and classrooms for breakout sessions," the Dean said. "You can also have our a/v equipment, the in-house technicians, and the Great Hall for receptions." This was great. Grant had solved multiple venue and technology problems. He felt he was off to the races.

The idea was to have everything in place in 18 months – from catering, to speakers, to a website where people could register and find the program. But as we talked about how to leverage the Dean's approval, Grant acknowledged that the Dean's underlying concern – money – was still a big factor. "I think the conference will pay for itself, maybe in three to five years as word spreads, but initially I'll need around $1 million. The private practitioners can pay their own way if they're speakers, but I'll have to pay for the government types and academics." So, once again, the question was how to find the resources.

A crucial element of leadership is knowing what resources you can call on; in what order to call on them so that each leverages the next; and how to make the most of each one as you access it. Here, Grant was a master. "I can use the Dean's approval," he said, "to get seed money from the General Counsel of [a giant drug company]. General Counsels like Deans – they see them as more practical than professors, who write articles that nobody reads." I smiled at the self-deprecating humor. Grant was charming. "Besides," he said, "I can convince this guy that his colleagues will learn more at the conference than in 200 hours of research. They can even learn what they *can't* from research – what's coming around the bend." So, the pitch would be efficiency.

All that remained was to wangle an appointment with a guy who flew around the world as often as he was in the office. "Oh, and here's the kicker," he said. "I'll put his company's logo on the website." Then he realized he didn't have a website. "I'd better get one designed pretty fast," he advised himself. "I can keep a few balls in the air." I didn't doubt that he could . . . especially since he reported at our next meeting that – while attending to all his other work – he'd had a Zoom call with the General Counsel. "This guy is sharp," he told me. "He'll draw up an MOU where he'll advance a million, then half of that, then half of that again over three years, provided we pick up the rest of the money from attendees and other sponsors." The GC was using discretionary funds. So, if he was using *his* resources, Grant reasoned that law firms would see the point and follow suit. "Heck, I'll put their logos on the website too. I'll make them feel part of this!"

But Grant realized that while he could leverage the drug company's example to encourage the law firms, they'd still probably demand some quid pro quo beyond supporting a great conference. "They know they'll learn stuff, and get advertising on our website, but they also want their lawyers to speak. They want real-time exposure, but that cheapens the conference – I'm opposed to pay-to-play." In insisting on the high road, however, had Grant limited his access to financial resources (apart from the paying attendees)?

He came up with the idea that potential speakers would compete for speakerships. "I'll invite everyone to submit ideas, and there will be an open-to-all discussion once they're submitted. We'll have an international pre-conferences on Zoom before decisions are made." Thus, he would inflect the conference with so much prestige that people would offer their best ideas and explain why they should present them. If they lost out to the competition – that is, if the fight was bruising but fair – how could anyone complain? They'd still be identified on the website with a prestigious conference (if there is one thing lawyers understand, it's competition). He'd also throw in a discount on conference tickets. So, problem solved.

But still. This was going to be a massive two-day conference with three tracks (Patents, Copyright, and Trademark), so how could he be sure to get all the best ideas from Zoom meetings, even assuming they were followed up by detailed written submissions (which he assumed that lawyers, being lawyers, would rush to provide)? How could he be sure that the ideas presented were as sound as their proponents claimed? "I need another resource for ideas, and to vet ideas" he told me. So, we discussed a plan he'd been contemplating for a while, basically to determine if it was practical. "You know," he said, "the students are overworked as it is – would they be willing to help organize this conference?" I said he wouldn't know unless he asked.

So, here came another elevator pitch. "I'll tell the kids in the IP Clinic that while it's great to help small local companies with advice on a trademark, or maybe a copyright infringement, wouldn't they like to be involved with issues – the cases and policies – that determine how IP is applied around the world? They'll get a sense of the global dimension of IP that they never get in class." So, he ordered in pizza and ice cream one afternoon (a sure draw in any law school), and invited everyone from the IP Clinic, as well as everyone else who was concentrating in IP (the law school had instituted concentrations to prepare students for practice in a particular field).

The students came. Many signed on. They agreed to listen to the Zoom calls, read the written submissions, and meet two or three times a week (in Patent, Trademark, and Copyright pods) as the suggestions began to roll in. They would help evaluate the suggestions, researching their background in the legal literature. But they would *also* research other potential ideas that no one had proposed. They would provide the intellectual backbone of the conference, authenticating every topic that ultimately made it into the program. It would be a heavy responsibility, but that's what the students actually wanted. "You know," he told me, "law students dream about real-world encounters with the law – it's why they join clinics, however small-potatoes the practice is. I'm appealing to that yen that they have to be closer to practice."

Grant had turned the students into a prime resource. He knew how to interest them, just as he knew how to interest the private firms that might not even get a speaking slot. He had organized the students into an effective resource by leveraging what they hoped to gain from the experience. If the private firms didn't always receive the quid pro quo they wanted, he was more than happy if the students did. "Okay, they're helping me, and I couldn't pursue this without them," he said, "but they're also learning. It's the best kind of law school experience, really – practical, stimulating, a great way to learn who the players are."

Once all the ideas were evaluated, and the best ideas finally chosen, the students could help to design the sessions – who would speak about what under a particular rubric. There might be sessions on emerging EU crackdowns on copyright infringement, or on the doctrine of "bad faith" in U.S. trademark law. Or how about an update on Big Pharma patents running out, only to be extended through technical tweaks? "I'm so close to this stuff," Grant told me, "and the students see it all with fresh eyes. They see patterns in the submissions, and in the results of their own research, that I might miss." In other words, the students provided *high-level* support and quality control, a resource that any conference – let alone one that staked a claim to prestige – could not do without. "I let the students know they're an indispensable resource. It's the best way to keep them coming back once they graduate and, in the meantime, to let them know that their hard work matters."

Grant approached his *human* resources respectfully. "If I'm going to lead this crew," he told me, "I can't treat them as cogs in a machine. If they're 'resources,' I still can't forget that they're people." I was impressed.

Of course, Grant still had to choose speakers for the plenary sessions (which looked at IP trends from a global perspective). These high-profile speakers would be the ultimate resource, big draws whose names everyone knew, who would attract paying attendees. So, Grant started issuing invitations. He made international visits (the drug company's grant paid for the trips). He obtained commitments from several. "Once I told an EU commissioner that his counterpart from the U.S. was speaking, I usually got a yes. But even when I got a no ("Your conference is too new – ask me again in the future"), he built up valuable connections. Connections *are* resources, however inchoate. Think of them as materializing in the future. At least, Grant did.

The rest of the organization and planning went pretty smoothly. "I'm going to record the proceedings, and then ask the students to edit and annotate them. I'll have to get the speakers' amendments, which can be a pain, but I think they'll like having their talks – their debates! – immortalized in a book." He lined up a legal publisher, whose books were regularly acquired by libraries. The book would also be available as an e-book – free to conference attendees on the website. "I want to make the conference itself a resource, which people can reference as they do their own research. Maybe we'll get cited in judicial opinions." Grant wanted the conference to go viral, so to speak, at least in a strict, soberly legal context. He wanted the conference to become self-sustaining because people wanted to sustain it, building on its success year after year.

Since the law school had a robust Continuing Legal Education (CLE) program, he could ensure that the conference offered CLE credits in accordance with its procedures. "That office is one more resource that I can't overlook," he told me. "They do a great job, so why invent the wheel?" Apparently, the law school even licensed conferences to other CLE providers, opening a major revenue stream to those who conducted them. It was a great deal! So, if Grant had to locate resources, he also knew when to use resources that readily came to hand.

As the conference took shape, Grant learned a lot about finding and utilizing resources. For example:

- Leaders leverage their resources, so that accessing one resource makes possible access to the next.
- Finding resources depends on knowing where to start – you can't leverage anything until there is something to leverage.
- When people are a potential resource, they will frequently demand a quid pro quo – the issue is whether to provide what they want, or deflect their demands by providing something else (the law firms wanted speaking slots, but got their logos on a prestigious, no-compromise conference).
- Sometimes imagination is called for, but other times you do not need to reinvent the wheel – it's important to know the difference.
- In order to get funded, you first must win over the people with funds.

Grant has held a couple of conferences since we began talking. He is not just piling up resources – like money, people, and venues – but is using them effectively.

***

The stories in this chapter demonstrate that planning and organization are not for the faint-hearted. Neither are they dry, green eye-shade pursuits for congenital bores. Rather, they are dynamic activities, on a par with finding your vision and pursuing it with determination. They require skill and a surprising amount of energy, since – unlike what they seem to be at first glance – they are not abstractions. That is, we tend (mistakenly) to think of "planning" as more or less like envisioning a future project, and we think of "organization" (mistakenly) in terms of charts that tend to display an administrative structure in two dimensions. But as the people in this chapter learn, planning and organization (as a dynamic duo) require constant attention and the ability to turn on a dime as situations evolve. They require imagination, an ability to project into the future, and a commitment to solving problems right now.

Frequently, we go back and forth between planning and organization as a project takes shape, as more people come on, as we learn what works and what doesn't. Thus, we may need to hire new people – an exercise of organization – because a plan did not work out as expected; they, in turn, may precipitate a change in plans. That's okay. It's all part of a learning process on the way to realizing some version of what we set out to do. Good organization will make our plans work (in some form); responsive planning will affect the organization we adopt (and may need to alter) as we attempt to follow through.

Some take-aways in this chapter include:

- Leaders take planning and organization seriously – the less left to chance the better.
- Planning and organization can last for the life of a project – there is no such thing as "set it and forget it" in complex undertakings, especially over a period of months or even years.
- When you attempt to lead a new project, expect that your plans – as well as your follow-through – will develop along with what you learn as well as in response to any unavoidable contingencies.
- Leaders not only know how to locate and use resources, but also the order in which they should best be utilized to achieve maximum impact.
- Administration is leadership by another name, since you are ensuring that all the moving parts in a project fit together and move in sync.
- Don't confuse planning with vision – plans help to achieve your vision, and may change more dramatically without affecting how what you've envisioned ultimately turns out.

While the people in these stories sometimes lost confidence in themselves, a good grasp of the planning and follow-through process helped to keep on them track. No matter how businesslike we may try to behave, in the end "leadership" is a personal pursuit. If we lack confidence, we'll be ineffective. Good planning and organization are an exceptional way to keep on keeping on, even in an unstable environment. They keep us steady. They offer a practical perspective on our dreams.

References

Hamilton (book, music, and lyrics by Lin-Manuel Miranda), 2015.

The Book of Mormon (book, music and lyrics by Trey Parker, Robert Lopez, and Matt Stone), 2011.

Chapter IV

Communication and Collaboration

We tend to think of communication and collaboration as natural outcomes of working together. As soon as two people (or a hundred or a thousand) start working in tandem, they necessarily talk, share information, and exert themselves towards some common objective. However, this is a misconception. It reduces the exchanges that we have with other people (some of whom we do not work with!) to a back-and-forth with no purpose other than enhancing each other's awareness – and, hence, of helping to get on with the job.

But effective communication and collaboration can be much more. By talking and sharing information, we change people's minds, excite them to join us, and encourage them to perform at a level that they could not have imagined on their own. In this sense, communication and collaboration are instrumental. They are strategic, and alter the landscape in our favor. The stories in this chapter illustrate how everyday leaders deploy communication and collaboration (which take a variety of forms) to create and promote new possibilities – literally, to change outcomes.

Everyday leaders rely on communication and collaboration as ongoing, extensible processes that can last for the entire duration of a project as it unfolds. These leaders are always learning, and listen as much as they send out directives or speak before their assembled employees. They understand that the process itself brings people closer, raising their spirits and level of commitment. Whatever else happens, they ensure that information flows in as many directions as may be necessary to keep on board and engaged. This type of sharing creates crucial, mutually supportive relationships.

Yet while this chapter addresses communication and collaboration together, it does not treat them as the same. That is, you can communicate without collaborating, though the former may (over time) give rise to the latter as people are drawn towards the same orbit. Communication that precedes collaboration will, of course, continue as the one gives way to the other. But in essence, when you communicate, you create an occasional relationship that does not require a shared objective; there may be one, though we often communicate with opponents. On the other hand, when you collaborate, there is always a common

DOI: 10.4324/9781003437635-5

objective, even though people may not agree on everything. Think of Republicans and Democrats – they fight internally, but members of each party share the overriding objective of gaining power.

Yet notwithstanding their different conceptual frameworks, communication and collaboration share some important features. For the everyday leader, both should be the product of careful calculation: what should I say? when? to whom? for what purpose? The opportunity to share information and ideas, and to learn from others, should never be approached casually. There will not be that many chances for a do-over, so it's important to do it right the first time and to make a good impression. Even as you learn by doing, consider every opportunity for an exchange as a type of elevator speech – get it right, and good things can develop for there.

Whether a situation involves communication and/or collaboration, the point is to create a type of synergy among people. These people develop habits of mind – in effect, they are trained – to act together *with you* in ways that would not otherwise have occurred. They may also be trained to act together in teams, producing a far greater impact than anyone might have on their own. Everyday leaders need to create such synergies, since their resources are often limited.

The stories in this chapter illustrate communication and collaboration in action, that is, in their active modes beyond mere information exchange. The leaders' ultimate objective is to engage people, and to raise their interest in a project. They do so creatively and economically, based on what they can offer in return.

Thus, in one story, a lawyer uses effective communication to advance a project within his firm, drawing his partners into an *ad hoc* collaboration. In another, a young woman learns how to deploy communication strategies to outflank the competition. Along the way, she discards strategies that worked in her family – but clearly do not in a wider, more impersonal, and less matriarchal environment. In still another story, an investment manager must convince his team (by using effective communication) that they ought to collaborate on a project that many may find uncomfortable. He does it by delivering an impressive pay-off. Other stories offer other, similarly nuanced examples.

So, as you read this chapter, consider some of these concerns:

- Both communication and collaboration are instruments of effective leadership, providing opportunities for a two-way exchange of information and ideas.
- They help leaders draw people closer to how such leaders hope such people will think.
- They create a type of synergism both within organized teams and on an *ad hoc* basis among people at large.
- Leaders should calculate how/when/to whom they intend to communicate, since do-overs are not always possible, and no opportunity should be wasted.
- Communication is an ongoing process, not just a one-off, and continues even after it gives way (if does) to a collaboration

The people in these stories are not experts in communication. Rather, they learn along the way. They discover that without effective communication and collaboration, they simply cannot succeed at effective leadership. Leaders are always generating ideas, and improving their ideas based on what they learn from others.

This story concerns a lawyer who uses collaboration strategically to consolidate his leadership position within the firm. Its point is that collaboration is not merely a necessity for "getting along" with other people, but rather an instrument for advancing one's own objectives – now and into the future. Collaboration is how you make things happen when they seem stalled or too inchoate to materialize. It's how you help people realize that collaborating with you is a two-way street, where they benefit as much as you do. So, as you read this story, ask yourself whether you fully understand the possibilities of collaboration, and can design a long-term program to collaborate effectively.

You might, for example, ask:

- *Have I thought through the parameters for collaboration in my own organization – what are the possibilities now and into the future?*
- *Whom do I need to work with more closely, and encourage to understand how my objectives can benefit them?*
- *Do I understand the language of collaboration, which is based in offering to help even as my own self-interest is a prime motivator?*
- *Is my sense of timing well-honed, so that I know when to be forthcoming?*

Collaboration is an art. It's not just a type of everyday give-and take so much as it is an ongoing, effective, evolving negotiation to get where you want to go. Learning how to collaborate is a crucial component of leadership because it helps you to retain and advance your position.

The Best Leaders Collaborate Strategically

Collaboration is like the Tide that Lifts all Boats

Before crypto-currency computers can be stacked together, or a wind farm built, or cell phone towers strung across mountains . . . somebody must invest billions of dollars. They must make deals. They sign contracts that run for hundreds of pages, stuffed with insurance riders, performance metrics, disclaimers, and provisos. That cell phone tower – which can rise 200 feet – is dwarfed by the vast legal effort required to build it. Hundreds of miles away in some glass tower (usually in Midtown Manhattan), lawyers draw up the terms that let the money flow. This conjunction of finance and critical infrastructure is a pivot point of capitalism. It's where my client Bill operates every day.

Bill, now in his late forties, is a partner at a top-tier Manhattan law firm, and Chair of the Global Infrastructure Finance Group. The Group, which accounts for almost 20% of the firm's profits, represents investment firms, portfolio companies, financial institutions, and multinational developers seeking to create, preserve, and enhance long-term interests in an array of complex infrastructure projects:

- Energy generation and transmission (solar, wind, hydro, and conventional) in the U.S. and abroad.
- Digital infrastructure (towers, data centers, wireless).
- Commodity pipelines.
- Oil and liquid natural gas tankers, drilling platforms and ships, and semi-submersibles.
- Mining, especially of rare metals.

Bill is expert across all phases of the underlying financial structure, from early project development to mergers and acquisitions (M&A). To date, he has led his group in transactions worth hundreds of billions of dollars across four continents.

So, why would this Master of the Universe need to talk with me about leadership? That he *did* need to, just proves that leaders want to promote the best organizational circumstances in which to lead. It's a combination of instinct and practicality. They know what's likely to work (chalk that up to experience and skill) and they can't bear conditions that are less than optimal. It's that drive to improve that got them where they are in the first place.

We began talking about three years ago. As we spoke, it emerged that while Bill was "Chair" of one of the firm's major components, that component was something of a mirage. "When I need support, I can call on lawyers from M&A, or Emerging Technologies, or even Banking," he said. "But it's always ad hoc, since my core group is relatively small." He described a group that felt kaleidoscopic, with lawyers cycling in and out depending on the nature of the transaction. They were never as singularly focused as he was; they never went out looking for business; their main responsibility was always to another group which generated most of their income. "I always feel like I'm sharing people," he told me, "like they're not really in the Group and I'm not really their leader." As a result, long-term strategies were harder to formulate and pursue. "I'm reduced to being an opportunist." In fact, he was often reduced to calling managing partners in the firm's overseas offices to plead for help on the ground.

So, Bill's real problem was that the firm's own infrastructure matched neither his ambitions nor his sense that financing major projects requires a large, dedicated team where the players know each other well, reinforce each other's strengths (and compensate for each other's weaknesses), and share the same long-term goals. "Clients don't want to keep seeing different faces," he said. "They want to ask for people by name – and they want people to know *their* names without being introduced." Translation: Bill wanted to lead a group that existed as a group, with defined contours and objectives. Of course, since the current structure was so profitable, he'd have to get the firm's hierarchy to change it.

We talked about how he could develop his own team, that is, how he could convince the firm that a dedicated team was better than one assembled from the firm's components as the need arose. I felt that this "mission" (as he called it) was a test of his leadership skills – he'd have to make a winning pitch, and bring people around to what he saw as best for the firm. "It's not like you're in enemy territory," I said. "This 'mission' is an exercise in collaboration – you're working with them, helping them understand what the financing of vast infrastructure projects needs on an extended timeline and across national boundaries."

I suggested that when Bill spoke with the Management Committee about allowing him to create this new, permanent group, he should choose his words from a vocabulary that evinced a desire to collaborate. "Maybe say something like 'I want to work this out together, so that we all benefit.' Or maybe 'I have my own ideas – but how do you envision this new group?'" In other words, it was important that Bill, as the leader of a diffuse group (who wanted to lead a coherent, wide-ranging, and successful group) act as though everyone was already on the same side. It was now just a matter of coming out where everyone was satisfied with the allocation of firm resources. Of course, Bill couldn't seem presumptuous ("I know I'm right, but you can fill in some details"). He could, however, actively listen, negotiate if he had to, and present a strong case while acknowledging everyone's interest in the outcome.

We spoke about collaborating from a position of strength. "Look," I said, "they have the ultimate say-so when it comes to letting you hire new people, but you bring in a huge chunk of the firm's income. Let them know you want to enhance the possibility of making that chunk bigger." Collaboration does not mean failing to take advantage of your own advantages in the interest of getting along. It does mean being strategic, and emphasizing how your strengths contribute to what could be a very successful shared project. Ultimately, you should find the right balance between what you can offer, and how other people's vision of the world should change in response to what you can offer. This is a form of strategic collaboration, which is much more nuanced (and thought-through) than a mere willingness to work together.

I suggested that Bill catalogue his greatest hits (e.g., the pipeline in Brazil, the new tanker fleet leased to an African nation), and explain how he scrambled to assemble a team (U.S.- and foreign-based) that pulled the deals together. "I'd let them know how much time and money the firm would have saved – and how much less it could have billed the clients for travel – if everyone had been at the ready." After all, Bill had enough business to justify a committed group of attorneys, so why prejudice the clients and the firm itself? "Ask them a rhetorical question," I said. "Get them to see how self-defeating any answer would be."

From a leadership perspective, effective collaboration requires effectively communicating your position. You help people see how, by working with you, they become part of a project that benefits them too. As I told Bill, "Collaboration starts as a two-way street, where you recognize what's coming from the other direction and help redirect it so that, in the end, you're all going in the same direction." It's a version of the famous book that they teach in business schools, *Getting to Yes: Negotiating Without Giving In.*

Bill and I did some mock "negotiations," where I was a partner skeptical of hiring more associates. I cited the additional cost and – as in any partnership – the need not to cause a stampede when all the partners suddenly demand parity. "Maybe they'll all want more associates, so they can establish their own fiefdoms," I said, trying to impersonate some old curmudgeon. But in each case, Bill had a response. "Why suppress one profit center," he asked, "just because others might as for support? The point is to allocate resources rationally." For Bill, the point was to challenge complacency while also showing concern for the firm's highest and best interest (profit). That interest, as he defined it, derived from rationally allocating resources. "I'm a *major* profit center," he said. "We have to emphasize what's working."

A few weeks later, the Committee came around, and agreed to allow him to hire three associates – all in finance, all with engineering backgrounds. Bill speculated that the stipulations allowed the Committee to feel as though it hadn't just given in (and to fend off other partners by explaining that Bill hadn't just received carte blanche). "But that's okay," Bill said. "I want them to feel like I'm collaborating, not just calling the shots." Smart move.

But Bill wasn't through. He went on what he called a "collaboration tour," designed to strengthen the Group's ties to strategically-placed partners in the firm's outlying offices – places like Los Angeles (a major transshipment point for Chinese imports) and Beijing (where most of those imports originated). "These guys aren't formally part of my Group," he said, "but I'll need to work with them as new projects develop. I want to establish reliable relationships." What I heard was that Bill sought to create a penumbra of people around his core group, populated by local experts on whom he could rely as the need arose. This was smart too. Bill was playing the game forward, in the sense that he *would* need these people – sometime – and wanted them to feel that they were *already* involved with his long-term objectives. Bill was offering prospects. In return, he was listening to these people, getting their ideas, even inviting them to call him when some likely project came over the transom. "I told them that the Group back in New York was always there for them – the implication being, of course, that we could call on each other."

Bill's idea of collaboration was ingenious. Even when there was nothing (yet!) to collaborate on, the glittering possibility encouraged people to think about each other, keep in touch, and finally collaborate in earnest when either of them perceived the advantage. Projects that might have been beyond the capacity of lawyers in outlying offices suddenly became plausible because everyone could call on each other for support. Projects that Bill originated, but that needed support in the field, now also became plausible. Bill's approach to collaboration drew on a networking model, but also expanded it by making future projects seem like a two-way exchange of leads and resources. He told me that "I see collaboration as relying on a measure of suggestion. I want people to think about collaborating so that, when the opportunity arises, the benefits are clear." In effect, Bill was creating a loosely integrated Group-to-be, which shared the same goals and only waited for them to become realizable.

After his tour, which was very hands-on and lasted several months, Bill reported back to the Management Committee. "I wanted them to know," he said, "that I was consolidating the firm, actually improving its functionality and likely profits." His ultimate objective was to join the Management Committee. He wanted to make policy and felt that his book of business, as well as the prospective book of business that he had created, was grounds for granting him a place.

Of course, Bill would not just come out and say "I deserve this! I'm a champion rain-maker." Again, we role-played, rehearsing a presentation based in the language of collaboration and firm-wide progress. Bill wanted to *link* collaboration and progress. He'd present himself as instrumental to a collaboration that would yield possibilities unlikely to otherwise develop. Bill would emphasize the future – the focus of his tour – and show how his approach to collaboration as a series of enhanced networks, would make for the bet future.

We are still refining his presentation. But during our conversations, and his putting into practice the ideas we discussed, Bill learned a lot about how to deploy collaborative techniques. For example:

- Collaboration is strategic, a give-and-take whose ultimate objective is to help you get where you want to.
- Leaders collaborate with other leaders (as Bill did with the Management Committee), presenting themselves as equals whose offer to help is a benefit to everyone.
- Collaboration is not just about the here-and-now. It's also focused on creating relationships that will be helpful in the future.
- The language of collaboration, that is, the type of communication that you deploy, should help people understand that you're on their side.
- It's hardly possible to lead unless you collaborate, since everyone has their own interests and you'll need to encourage them to work with you towards your goals.

Bill operates in an environment where everyone has a major ego, and wants to be seen as an effective leader as much as Bill wants to actually be one. His collaborative skills will be crucial to navigating his situation (as he knows all too well). By carefully practicing his collaborative initiatives, he can make the most of his skills – and, thus, of his potential as a leader.

The following story concerns a young woman who discovers her calling only gradually, and discovers how to make the most of it through creative collaborations. She also arranges ad hoc collaborations, strategically communicating with people outside her organization who (for their own reasons) may want to help her. She learns that effective leadership requires constant conversations on many fronts.

So, as you read this story, ask yourself:

- *Do I see collaboration as a means of eliciting information, even if I don't necessarily want to take all of it?*
- *Do I know how to interest people in my objectives, and how to encourage them to address them candidly?*
- *Do I make time in every day to think about what I have learned from other people, and not just from my own experience?*
- *Am I willing to widen my perspective to take seriously what other people have to tell me?*

The woman in this story had to think about these questions during the formative year of her business. Because she learned how to answer them with Yes, the business took off.

Leaders Turn Everyone into Collaborators

When You Find Someone who May Know Something, Don't Be too Shy to Ask

Not everyone who *can* be a doctor thinks that they should be. My client Lilly is an example. By the time she arrived at college, she had already satisfied most pre-med requirements through a combination of AP courses and selective early enrollments. By any standard, she was on a glide path to medical school. "I could just show up *now*," she used to joke, "and they'd let me in." But that was then. By junior year, medical school – and being a doctor – seemed like just more of the same. "Not a challenge," she told a professor. "I want something that keeps me up at night." She wanted what didn't come easily. Her guidance counselor said to take a year off and try something completely different. "Clear your head," he said. "Challenge yourself in new ways." She did, and it changed her life.

Lilly moved back to rural Oregon, where her sister (who was 180° opposite Lilly) lived in a collective that grew an heirloom wheat that thrived in the arid climate. It also grew grapes which, when the harvest was good, were pressed into wine that was sold to local restaurants. "I thought I'd have time to think," Lilly told me, "and to help out my sister who is dyslexic." Little did she realize how the experience would affect her.

Within a month, Lilly had figured out that the collective's kitchen – where she'd been assigned to the bread-baking detail – was grossly inefficient. She told me "they were making sourdough starter from wheat tailings, when there was natural yeast in the air . . . on the apple trees, even on the grapes before they were pressed." As part of her kitchen duties (and to relieve her frustration) Lilly wrote a sort of elementary cookbook, demonstrating how to make sourdough from natural starters. She called it "Efficient Baking – Saving Your Resources and Reducing Your Work." Lilly's dyslexic sister, Rosie, made the accompanying detailed drawings.

Of course, the book was a hit. The kitchen staff asked Lilly to tutor them in the basic chemistry of bread, which was laid out in the book but was still a little hard for most people to apply. Lilly complied. "You know," she told me, "I actually enjoyed tutoring, and the people were so responsive." The experience got Lilly thinking.

Lilly thought that in the rural community outside the collective, lots of people might welcome learning how to bake from natural yeasts. So, for a few hours a week, she taught a course open to anyone on the chemistry of bread. "It was bi-weekly for four weeks, and the collective charged $100. People got to keep the bread they made, so they had an incentive to learn," she told me. More importantly, Lilly had begun to see a different future for herself. In effect, she could take what she was good at – the chemistry of living things – and turn it into a profession that wasn't Being A Doctor. This seemed like a true challenge. She'd have to design a career that relied on what she knew but that brought her to a new, more interesting place. She could see herself tutoring people in subjects that *they* thought were hard, and were willing to pay her to explain.

When Lilly returned to college for her senior year, she switched out of pre-med (where she had satisfied all the requirements anyway) and started taking courses in educational technology. She also took a course on psychology, on the assumption that if she was going to tutor for a living, she'd better understand how people respond to someone who knows more than they do. "I didn't want to teach classes," she told me. "I wanted to work one-on-one so that people could learn at their own pace and really get to like a subject." Okay, that part about liking a subject may have been idealistic, but Lilly was still firming up a vision of how she could apply her scientific knowledge in a setting that was interesting and challenging. The challenge would come from organizing a tutoring project that was self-sustaining – unlike living in the collective, she knew she would have to make a living.

So, during her senior year in college, Lilly started a company, "Accessible Tutoring," which offered in-person help to anyone having trouble with math, chemistry, biochemistry, or physics (all the pre-med subjects that she had aced). Just for fun, she threw in culinary chemistry, hoping to attract amateur bakers.

She put up flyers around campus, and at the off-campus laundromat. She put up a website announcing her personalized approach:

> I work directly with you. I get to know you, and we'll go at a pace that is comfortable for you. Even if you have OCD, ACHD, or dyslexia, I can help. You will learn and not just memorize. You will feel better about yourself, and perform better when it's crunch time.

Overnight, Lilly was inundated. Pre-med students signed up *en masse* based on Lilly's reputation. Local moms registered their kids. Even local bakers wanted to see what Lilly could show them. The demand got so intense that Lilly found herself tutoring 25 hours a week and on Sundays. She was afraid of burning out. "At one point," she told me, "I was afraid that I wouldn't graduate. I took a week off and went back to the collective, where I talked to people whom I trusted." Lilly finally concluded that while she had found a calling, she would have to organize her work on a different basis.

Of course, Lilly did graduate. She moved to New York and, after setting up without the obligations of her own studies (and watching the number of her clients hit the max) she came to see me.

As we began to talk, it emerged that while Lilly had conceived of tutoring as a relationship, the relationship was always with *her*. She was the linchpin of "Accessible Tutoring," implying that people would always have access to Lilly herself. So, I suggested that Lilly revise her definition of "accessible" to mean We Make The Subjects Accessible. That way, Lilly could hire other tutors, and still maintain her basic ethos of one-on-one tutoring – just not always with Lilly. The idea appealed to her . . . until she realized that she would have to train and supervise anyone she hired. "How am I supposed to do that and still do what I want to, which is to spend my time tutoring?"

I explained that she could do both, and that after a while the people whom she trained would be more like collaborators than trainees. "They'll learn the model – the one-on-oneness of what you do. They'll probably even have good ideas."

So, Lilly called up a few friends from college who had taken a gap year before graduate school. "How'd you like to work with kids – and with me – on a project that will burnish your c.v.? You can help me build it while you earn some money." Three people were interested, and Lilly was off to the races. Suddenly, she had gone from a tutor plastering stickers on lamp posts, to being a C.E.O. She was the leader of a tutoring company, with a clientele aspiring to improve their S.A.T.s and MCATs. "It was a little dizzying," she told me. "I studied the websites of other tutoring companies because now I was their competitor." One of the first things leaders realize is that, if their company is to succeed, it must learn from and outsmart the competition. "I wasn't trying to be as big as they were, or even to copy them, but I had to offer a service that made people choose me over them."

We talked about what Accessible Tutoring could do to be *more* accessible. That was a good way of competing, I said. I suggested that Lilly seek advice from the new tutors who, I thought, might not yet feel fully integrated into the operational side of the business. "Why don't you have weekly meetings, and make them feel like real collaborators? You should elicit their ideas about the business." In effect, they could tutor each other.

Lilly liked the idea.

One tutor, Jeremy, said that accessibility meant that even if people were handicapped, or on vacation or traveling, or even if they kept odd hours because they had other obligations, Accessible Tutoring could be there for them – virtually! He suggested that the company move its operations online, so that tutors could tailor their schedules to meet the clients'. This would also save the cost of renting space, since each tutor could operate from their own digs. "The money we save," he said, "could go back into the business."

Lilly told me that she thought the idea was terrific, but that she would give people the option of in-person or remote tutoring. Nonetheless, she said that she could see the merit of turning employees into collaborators. "I also decided to give them a stake in the business, a sort of profit-sharing arrangement." Also, some tutors were in exceptionally high demand, and she wanted to recognize them.

As the weekly meetings continued, other ideas emerged. "I know we specialize in STEM subjects," one guy said, "but how about tennis, or sailing?" He had been a member of their college tennis team, and learned to sail during summers on Cape Cod. So, why not offer lessons? Again, Lilly was intrigued, though she worried about liability insurance where a physical activity was involved. But finally, she bought a policy and had a lawyer draw up a hold-harmless agreement. "I realized," she told me, "that being 'accessible' means helping people to access skills that aren't just those that every tutoring service teaches. We can help them access another side of themselves." This would be especially helpful for special-needs kids with coordination and motor skill deficits.

In fact, the whole idea of physical activity ultimately led Lilly to include Tae Chi and yoga, a breakthrough in the tutoring space.

Lilly could not have offered what her website called Whole Person Training without her team-wide collaboration, which she now actively pursued. "It's really become a feedback loop," she told me. I teach them my ethos of in-person, up-close-and-personal interaction, and they give me ideas on how to improve on that. In other words, for Lilly, collaboration had become a means of mutual exchange where – even as a leader or, especially, because she was a leader – she learned from everyone with whom she worked. By collaborating, Lilly was defining her company – not just by making "accessible" more resonant, but by establishing new ways to deliver tutoring services and new subjects to offer. "I feel," she said, "that collaboration in this context is a type of reverse mentoring, where we all raise each other's potential."

As we continued talking about the company, I observed that while Lilly was excited about collaborating, the effort was still largely internal. "How about reaching out," I suggested, "and getting parents or teachers involved? They could tell you a lot that's not apparent even in in-person one-on-one sessions." I had in mind a child's work habits, or whether they needed extra support to raise their self-esteem. Maybe they were worried about the SATs, in which case a tutor's might talk about their own experience. "Communication is a form of arm's length collaboration – the people don't work *with* you, at least formally, but they can provide information that helps achieve a mutual objective." Communication is *ad hoc,* but you can call on people when they're useful. Most of the time, they want to be useful, if only you just ask.

"It's funny," I said, "how most people don't even realize they have useful information. But once you get them talking, you can elicit it." I observed that Lilly's clients would have "access" to more help if she – and their tutors – had greater access to how those clients processed information and felt about their prospects. This was especially true because most clients never mentioned their weaknesses to the tutors ("I don't want those geniuses to think I'm dumb"). But, as I told her, part of leading an organization is to look outside it, and draw on the knowledge of people who, though they're peripheral, can still provide an important perspective.

So, Lilly put up a page on her website for parents and teachers to make appointments to talk about any of the students. They could talk with Lilly herself or any of the tutors.

Of course, the requests flooded in, and I asked whether these conversations (which Lilly described as "candid") had led to any noticeable improvement in students' performance. "I think," she said, "that the tutors are better equipped to spot why a student may not be catching on. They're better able to approach problems, especially so that students don't feel defensive." Apparently, Lilly's attempt to communicate outside the confines of the organization – to deputize the parents and teachers – was having a positive effect.

Lilly also told me that by talking with parents, she learned that several older kids needed help writing a personal essay as part of their college applications. The kids had never said anything. So, Lilly started to offer on-on-one tutorials on How to Figure Out What Makes You Unique, and what would appeal to college admissions officers. These tutorials were hit and, Lilly told me, "I expanded my services just by talking with people. It turned out to be a great MO."

So, during the year or so that we spoke about Accessible Tutoring, Lilly enhanced her own access to individuals – inside and beyond the company – who could help her. She did it by collaborating with her employees (she now referred to them as her "team"), and communicating with other people who became part-time, occasional, quasi-collaborators. "I think," she told me, "that I have to regard everyone as a potential resource." She has even started eliciting feedback from the students ("not of the Rate My Professor variety, but just to gain another perspective on how we're doing").

As she evaluated her leadership experience to date, Lilly learned (among many things) that:

- Collaboration with your employees is a learning experience, and it multiplies your chances to complete effectively.
- Communication with those on the periphery of your organization turns them into *ad hoc* collaborators.

- You can expand our business by learning information about your clients that they may not reveal on their own.
- People enjoy helping you think about your business – they rarely see your request as an imposition, and may even see a benefit to themselves.

For Lilly, leadership during the formative stages of Accessible Tutorials became an exercise in eliciting useful information. She had to interpret it, of course, and determine how to apply it (for example, she didn't just abandon in-person for virtual meetings, though she liked the idea of providing increased access). She was still in charge, and the buck stopped with her. But she could use the information she acquired to make judgments about what moves should be next and when to make them. "I don't mind being tutored myself," she laughed.

This story concerns a woman who applies the model of her family relationships to how she pursues her business career. Of course, she learns that there are better means of becoming a successful leader. Most importantly, she learns how to deploy communication strategically, so that she outflanks the competition. She learns that competition need not produce zero-sum results, and that consensus may come at a price she is unwilling to pay.

So, as you read this, ask yourself these questions:

- *Do I understand leadership as a type of Darwinian struggle? Hint: that's probably not the best approach.*
- *Do I communicate in a way that leaves the competition no room to outflank me?*
- *As a leader, do I understand that successful performance is a better means of competition than confrontation?*
- *Am I able to sustain useful relationships through effective, ongoing communication?*

The woman in this story finally gets the right answer to these questions, but only after shedding some ingrained preconceptions.

Compete or Communicate?

For the Best Leaders, it's not an Either/Or Proposition

The first thing Carlita did when she came to New York from Peru was to introduce herself as Carly. "I wanted to skip all those questions like 'Where are you from?' (she said, as I asked where she was from), and just get to the heart of any matter." In other words, Carly shifted the focus away from herself towards a kind of instant mutuality. "I hate making things about me," she said, reflecting what she called a need to inhabit a shared space. Her large immigrant family, where everyone had pulled together, was her model for how to conduct her life. "I lost my accent," she told me, "but not my essential modus operandi."

Clearly, Carly had thought about how to conduct relationships. Her intense, personal experience (grounded in her family's experience) inflected how she made her way in the world. She and her sister had worked starting in high school, and parceled out expenses with their mother. Their father, on disability, had become an expense as well. "I can't imagine," she said, "not moving through life as a team."

So, as we spoke, I sensed that my role would be to sharpen her instincts – which homed in on shared, useful communication – rather than to help her acquire new skills. She already *knew* how to conduct a conversation so that no one felt ill at ease, dominated, bored, or at risk of wasting their time. Our work together, I thought, would boil down to ensuring that she could establish professional relationships that (while they might morph over time) could survive the hard knocks of life outside a family that supported each other.

Carly confirmed my sense by announcing, "I've entered a new phase of my career. I want to be sure that when I talk, people stay engaged." What she meant, I learned, was that she wanted to hold people's attention irrespective of any competing distractions. "We may not be one big, happy family," she said, "but I want to feel that the people I work with are pulling together in the same direction." She wanted, I thought, to call the shots in an environment where other voices and other incentives might pull people in various, not always compatible directions.

Echoes of a matriarchy? Of her *family's* accidental matriarchy? I would offer her the benefit of a provisional doubt. We started with her recent history.

By the time she graduated college, Carly was already politically active. She had worked part-time in the office of the Bronx Borough President. She met the right people, she said, and had even dated a few. "I got my name in Page Six," she grinned, "but I liked the publicity. I never missed a chance to meet people." I thought she was attracted to powerful men, sort of stand-in for her disabled father. But clearly, she understood how the game was played, and seemed to enjoy the hustle.

The game paid off.

Carly's first big break was her appointment as Director of Community Affairs for a New York State representative. "I made the transition from city to state, which meant a lot more exposure – you get the distinction, don't you, between 'publicity' and exposure?" I assumed she meant that the whiff of trading sexual favors was now behind her. I smiled, but didn't ask. But I did get a sense that she knew what she wanted and was willing to go after it.

In any case, Carly's new job required that she travel the state, meet local leaders, and urge them to support policies coming up for a vote in Albany. "I had to make them appreciate what we were doing, and see how it helped their constituents. Then I had to lock in their support." It was genteel horse-trading, since Carly had to intimate – without explicitly promising – that their support would be reciprocated (sometime, anyway). It was the type of politics that New York had made famous. Carly loved it. It flattered her ego. Maybe, even, it boosted her sense that she could deploy her sex appeal without being overtly sexy. But as she put it, "it tested my ability to communicate. I felt that we were all on the same page."

For Carly, communication meant corralling people into a shared space. It was not bullying, much less handing down *ex cathedra* directives. It was simply a mode of ensuring that everyone got along on terms that she felt were reasonable, productive, and ideally far-sighted. She liked to be the instrument of a durable consensus. Still, I wondered whether in the "new phase" of her career for which had come to see me, this attitude of subtly but firmly calling the shots was likely to pay off.

In state government, it had worked spectacularly. Apparently, she was so good at lining up local officials behind Albany's latest proposals – that is, at straddling the fence between vagueness and reassurance – that she caught the eye of the Governor. He appointed her to a task force overseeing highway upgrades, a hot topic since some upstate roads washed out during a storm. "Maybe I could have run for something myself," she said, "and I almost took the plunge."

That is, until an even bigger opportunity (the one that landed her in my office) suddenly came along.

The capitalists found her. One evening, during a reception at the Governor's mansion, the head of a major telecom company asked if she would work for him. "I was startled," she told me. "I had never thought of myself as a corporate type. I liked building alliances – not backstabbing." But the job on offer *required* that she build relationships. "It was," she said, "not so different from what I had been doing – but the scale was so enhanced, that it *was* different."

The position, Vice President of Government Affairs, would ensure that city, county, and state officials nationwide were receptive to (and would pave the way for) the company's expansion. The company – among the largest providers of shared wireless infrastructure – needed rights of way, easements, zoning variances, and a host of red-tape abatements so that cell towers could go up without local (read: NIMBY) opposition. Carly, who was still just 35, took the job and, that very day, made an appointment to see me.

So, what exactly did she want to discuss? An apparent paradox. Instead of communicating with officials outside her immediate environment – that is, external to the Governor's office – she now faced powerful players who were, ostensibly, on the same side. But only ostensibly. "They all think they're calling the shots," she said. "They're like individual power centers and they all want to persuade each other (including me)." In effect, they all had personal ambitions within the company, and advanced their own views to promote their ambitions. Nobody lined up behind anybody, at least without a fight. So, Carly's ideal of orchestrating a durable consensus was now challenged by a kaleidoscope of opinion, with everyone as determined as she was. "How can I go out and represent the company – even politely twist arms – if I don't have support in the C-Suite?" she asked.

She answered her own question by sighing "I'm too busy fighting a rearguard action."

I thought she was still settling in, and that things would finally calm down. But, as we spoke, I realized that Carly's problem – as she perceived it – was an extension of how she viewed success. She always needed to be on top. When she worked for the state, she led a small staff and reported directly to the Governor. She'd had no rivals. But now she was part of a team of rivals, all vying in their separate spheres to get noticed, praised, and promoted. Carly hated all the jockeying. "I can't even lead my own team of Government Affairs experts if I have to make sure that no one else sucks up the oxygen around me," she said.

I knew this personality type. Carly tended to view leadership as a zero-sum game, where everyone else's drive for success undermined her own. From her perspective, someone always threatened to cross into her lane, and she had to nudge them back. So, I explained that leadership required an open mind. You need to listen. "But," she insisted, "they all think they can do my job better than I can." I knew this refrain too. So, I responded, "No, that's not really it. They would hate taking on your responsibilities, but they want to be acknowledged." Part of leadership, I suggested, is to effectively communicate your position, listen attentively, and then hold your ground (except where you affirmatively chose to make an accommodation). If you take on board someone else's ideas, then acknowledge them. But it's not your job to lead everyone outside your chain of command so that fall in behind you. They can jump and scream all they want. You just need to get on with your work.

In effect, I was urging Carly not to see the world – or, rather, the corporate world – in terms of protracted competition. "Though you and your team don't inhabit a silo," I said, "you can't let yourself worry about other people's ambitions." Besides, I felt that Carly projected onto other people her own ambitions, in a toxic feedback loop. So no wonder the race felt intractable – even inescapable – given her own ingrained ambition. I thought that instead she should focus on producing results with her own team. "Your results will speak for themselves," I said. "If you get a raise or a promotion, it will be on account of those results – just as it always has been." For a leader, results stand in for competition. They say everything about you without your having to say anything.

From this perspective, leadership requires a certain inward-facing, where you concentrate on making your team as effective as possible. "Communicate with *them*," I said, "rather than trying to persuade unpersuadable Suits who do not answer to you." In effect, stay in your lane, and be sure that everyone behind you gets the right message.

So, we spoke about how Carly could train and supervise her staff, and how they could strategize together. "Cement your team," I suggested. "Make them feel part of your efforts by *explaining* stuff." I said that intra-team communication was just as important as – in fact, more important than – protecting her flank, since she would ultimately be judged on her performance.

How could Carly enhance that performance? Her idea was to encourage state governments to lease the company's technology to enhance wireless reception in underserved communities. "The contracts," she said, "could be worth billions out to the next decade, especially if you add in maintenance. If I could close even one, I'd get a promotion." The only hitch (and it was big) was that she'd need approval from the Suits to pursue any deal of that magnitude (could the supply chain handle it? would other business have to be diverted? would new personnel need to be hired?). The same people who infuriated her when she first arrived, would now be able to raise all sorts of seemingly reasonable objections.

So, we talked about how to get past them. She'd write a White Paper, "Opportunities for Wireless and Satellite Services in Underserved Rural Areas," which she would circulate internally. She would produce a companion PowerPoint presentation, and invite the Suits to have their say. Her M.O. would be a type of hyper-communication intended to outflank the opposition by anticipating (and effectively answering) their questions. She'd have all the numbers. She'd delineate all the benefits and name names of government officials whom she knew would be receptive. She'd bring her entire team along as back-up to answer any questions where she didn't have the data at her fingertips.

Leadership, I told her, involves making your case to skeptics, leaving them no room to object except out of petulance. It's a type of forward-looking communication that responds to objections *before* they are raised.

Ultimately, she was successful, at least internally. Then she began her campaign with the states. To back her up, the company went into overdrive, taking out full-page ads in the *Times* and *Wall Street Journal* about how they could bring woe-begone areas into the 21st century. The company's stock went up. Carly got a promotion.

"I owe all this," she told one interviewer, "to effective communication." But what she really meant was that she'd learned how to deploy the forms of soft competition. She prepared her team, kept them in the loop, and made sure that no one could rationally stand in her way. When she had previously tried to compete with the Suits, she had not anticipated their potential objections. Nor had she thought that there was room for Herself and Them in the same corporate boxing ring. Now, however, she displayed a different attitude. "I out-thought them," she told me. "It wasn't that we all formed a consensus so much as that they just got out of the way." She neutralized them rather than persuading them, all by means of limiting what they could say that would counter what she said. It was a subtle, but crucial difference.

As if she needed any affirmation, *Forbes* named her in its "40 Under 40" list. She was up-and-coming. Her college put her on the Board of Overseers, and the Rural Alliance named her "Woman of the Year." But what was most important, was that she finally ditched her self-absorbed idea of how competition works in a corporate setting. Here are some of the things she learned:

- When faced with internal jockeying, the best leader will keep her head down and focus on her team.
- Performance speaks for itself, and is the best form of competition.
- Rather than overtly competing, the best leader outflanks the competition through a type of hyper-communication which leaves the opposition with no effective come-back.
- The model of consensus that you may have learned in your family does not necessarily translate to a setting where there are no emotional ties to smooth over grievances.

Carly is still working at the telecom, and now leads the charge to install wireless technology. She continues to make contacts. "I'm creating a neural network of relationships," she says, "because we're all responsive to each other. I can't imagine doing this on my own."

This story concerns an investment manager who decides to reinvent the practice of investment banking. He wants to introduce ideas that may seem (at best) tangential, but which he regards as potentially transformative. As a leader, he must convince his team to collaborate in applying these ideas, even though they may make some team members uncomfortable.

So, as you read this story, ask yourself:

- *Can I, through my own example, demonstrate the value of applying new ideas?*
- *Do I collaborate in ways that foster trust between team members, and the team and myself?*
- *Do I know how to erect guardrails, so that my team does not feel threatened by new ideas, and want to try them?*
- *Am I good at evaluating the impact of new ideas, so that I don't just casually spring them on people who are not ready for them?*

The manager in this story was able to answer these questions affirmatively, but also continually evaluated his progress. "You can't lead," he said, "without doubling back on what you've done. You should make sure that you're working at your peak." See how he does it.

Pushing the Envelope of what's Possible

Collaboration Requires Conviction, but also Reassessment

When Mitch walked into my office, I thought of that old saw, "What do you give someone who has everything?" Mitch, around 50, was at the top of his game. He ran an investment management service for high net-worth families with multigenerational wealth. His typical client was not a person, but a whole family with staggering numbers of zeroes backing up their disposable capital. So, I could only ask, "Hey, what's the problem?" Not surprisingly, he admitted, "I'm not sure. I even like what I do." But believe it or not, that was a start.

When people approach me with an indefinable problem, I interpret that as their belief (however inchoate) that there is more to do. The question is: "*What* to do?" As we began talking, Mitch struck me as a striver. He had held positions in increasingly large investment banks, handling increasingly large portfolios for an increasingly large number of clients. "It was only natural," he told me, "that at some point I'd form my own management company. I did, and my clients just followed me." But strivers are restless. They believe the Next Big Thing is *always* out there. Mitch had put that belief into practice. . . and now, even with his own firm, he was restless for what was Next.

"What would you do if you could?" I asked. "Assume the only limitation is your ability to imagine it."

As it turned out, Mitch did not want to keep running the firm he had started. He wanted to found and lead a new firm, based on principles that he wanted to test. These principles, which he loosely codified as Radical Collaboration, showed the way to reinvent (so he insisted) the practice of wealth management. Reinvent? I recalled another old saw, "If it ain't broke, don't fix it."

But Mitch was serious. He wanted to create something less impersonal, more organic, alive, and responsive to human instincts that (he insisted) really drive the market. He wanted to add a new dimension to market analysis that encompassed an analyst's humanity. I couldn't imagine what he meant. But when he registered my expression, he was started laying it out.

"Right now," he explained, "my team crunches numbers, but it's not enough." In addition to charts and forecasts, he envisioned a model beyond the purview of business schools. "This is definitely extracurricular," he said, grinning.

I tried not to appear skeptical. But still, I had to ask if this unconventional approach was risky.

"I'm not going soft," he told me. "I just think that an important element – the human element – is left out of our equation." His reinvented approach would, it seemed, be only *somewhat* unconventional. That is, it *would* be numerical, but not exclusively. He would improve on using numbers, not discard them.

I asked him to tell me more. "For one thing, 'management' will not be top-down. There'll be real, give-and-take among my team." Mitch saw his *team* as a kind of family. "If you can't bare your soul to people you work with," he said, "they won't understand your motivations, and why you think money should go here and not there. The best investment decisions turn on trust and understanding." Depending on how this soul-baring worked, it would or wouldn't work. If it meant that people were unafraid to discuss their hunches, and didn't shrink from critiquing other people's hunches, then it might be effective.

I do not discourage clients from thinking outside the box, so I reserved judgment. I simply advised Mitch to take care before he took the plunge.

He took the plunge, taking several buddies with him to a new firm that he called Aspiration, Inc. "I explained my new direction to them. It was my first test of Radical Collaboration, and it passed." What he meant, was that he had been totally candid, exposing his need to pursue a life in business continuous with the rest of his life. "I told them that choosing investments is no different from how you connect with people – you find ones that you identify with, and that make you feel energized. You find ones that excite your sense of possibility." They bought it. "I wanted to come off as real, and give them permission to be the same with me." He hoped their collaboration would, going forward, be as open as he had been.

But he went forward on his own, revealing even more of himself. "I admitted that after years in therapy, I finally realized that living with a sense of possibility was the only way to save my marriage. I've been restless, always focused on change, not growth – possibility can lead to growth." He had learned to make this vital distinction, and acknowledged why it was important. He bared his soul, which was basic to Radical Collaboration. He described in unmistakable, vivid terms, how he wanted to proceed through life and connect the process to how he would pick investments. "I wanted them to follow my example as we set out together in making Aspiration a new kind of investment firm."

He made a video of his presentation ("It stunned my wife"), and he sent it to his old clients. About half signed on with the new venture. "That's about what I expected," he told me. "The smart ones realized that if I'm true to myself, I'll be honest with them."

We kept talking as Aspiration picked up the pace of investing. The team was now holding weekly sessions, explaining why they liked one investment over another. The numbers jostled with more personal motivations. "I'm leading by example," he said, as we discussed those sessions. "People know their psychology matters, and that no motivation is off-limits." The point was to clarify team members' previously hidden rationales. If someone had a bad experience buying a house, the team should know, so it could evaluate why a member resisted investing in an REIT (real estate investment trust). If someone hated corn flakes because that's all there was for breakfast at prep school, that might explain their aversion to buying into an agricultural conglomerate. "Once we all know this stuff, we can make rational decisions together."

"But isn't there a risk?" I asked. "People may feel like they're under a microscope – like they're sacrificing their privacy." Mitch said No, so long as everyone participated equally. "I want to lead by leveling," he told me, "and I'll be the first to be leveled by what I say about myself." It sounded more like group therapy than an investment strategy, but the proof would be in whether they beat the market. If their clients got richer, and the team got bigger bonuses, then it *could* be a strategy – provided everyone kept up the self-revelation.

So, we kept talking. Mitch's goal was to demonstrate why collaboration requires that you explore seemingly unrelated or, at best, tangential issues that may turn out to be central. "If I am going to lead," he told me, "I have to convince people around me to try new, potentially effective approaches." Mitch saw leadership as a shared attempt to break through to new insights, and new ways of approaching problems. He was trying to make his own insight – that finance is driven by personal experience – into a shared, demonstrable, workable conviction that would (in time) become a practical *modus operandi*. He said, "I want to create an ecosystem, a new set of principles that keeps working for people so they keep buying into it." He wanted his team to open up because they saw a reason to explain who they were, and how that influenced their thinking. Why, for example, did someone shudder at taking a calculated risk, or (conversely) feel gung-ho towards a new opportunity? Put this way, the idea made sense.

I recognized the basic approach, which resonated with popular claims that psychology had a place in business. Only here, it seemed more concrete or, at least, subject to the ultimate test of how it impacted the bottom line. I recalled the legendary Ray Dalio, who founded Bridgewater on the idea of "radical transparency," where its leaders knew the personal histories of many employees. In Aspiration, everyone would know everyone else's personal histories, and accept them because there was no other choice. "Are we for real or not?" he asked. Mitch said he would lead the group toward a new kind of collectivity, where shame was factored out. "We're not judging each other," he said, "just objectively evaluating each other's judgment."

So, was it working out that way? At the weekly meetings, a team member would present a project, in financial but also in personal terms (why, for example, personal concerns made the project attractive). Then, during the following week's meeting, everyone would offer personal reasons supporting or rejecting it. Mitch said that things got pretty dramatic. "We broached concerns about incentive and motivation, and why someone might feel inhibited. No one called anyone's feelings illegitimate – just ill-advised, or maybe misplaced in context with the project at hand." It sounded adult (Mitch liked the term "highly evolved"). At the very least, people respected each other's research, augmented by their personal stance on it.

So, Mitch called himself a facilitator, standing back and encouraging discussion. "Okay," he said, "I'm the leader. But my goal is to broker consensus through clarity and insight." In effect, he'd adopted the mantle of leader-as-guru – a little grandiose, perhaps, but at the same time sort of humble. The ideal was always to understand, to reach what became known in these sessions as the Big Why.

Of course, there were hiccups, what a trained psychologist would have called doubts and insecurities. I wondered whether Mitch, who had an MBA, was presumptuous in subjecting people to all this – the self-revelation and critiques – without professional training. He thought not ("Hey, I'm nothing if not self-aware"). But on reflection, he agreed that a psychologist might provide guardrails. So, he hired one who would intervene if the conversation took an unsettling turn. The hope was that people would be less inhibited if someone were monitoring their safety. The psychologist signed the same NDA as everyone else, so there would be no leaks.

Nonetheless, during what we both identified as the "hiccup stage," it was never certain what might transpire. One woman, working on a real estate deal, broke down over how her family ruined itself by trying to flip unmarketable houses. "They showed crazy judgment," she told Mitch, "and now I'm terrified of anything related to real estate." A guy admitted that he and his wife fight over buying growth stocks ("We need the money now," she'd insist), and the strain was so awful that he shrank from a similar discussion among his peers. "I decided to hold our meetings in the afternoon," Mitch told me, "so I wouldn't be demoralized for the rest of the day."

But with it all, I was coming around to his point of view. If you're pushing the envelope, the envelope may sometimes push back. A good leader learns how far and how fast to push, and how to interpret the push-back. Mitch felt that it was worth persevering with Radical Collaboration, no matter the strain on himself and some of his team. Crucially, no one quit. No one rebelled. No one even asked that he go easier, which led Mitch to believe that the team was coming around. The quarterly reports didn't lie. "This first quarter," Mitch told me, "we beat the Russell 3000 by 24%."

Mitch said that *radical* collaboration meant that you got to the root of a working relationship, and made it work from the ground up. You understood how and why it worked, so you could fix it if something failed to work. "My goal," he said, "is to have a unified mental process where, ultimately, we think like one person would think. We weigh all our concerns internally, and then we decide." I wondered whether a team could replicate the internal rumination of a complex human being with complex emotions and years of personal history. But Mitch had it as a goal. He was still a striver.

Over the next several months, the team worked towards a balance of how much to share – it couldn't be *so* much that each individual became the focus rather than the project at hand. That would be counter-productive and, as a leader, Mitch saw it as his role to keep the firm moving forward. "I was a rower in college," he told me, "and I learned that you win when everyone stays in sync."

I thought that rowing was a good model, especially because everyone must also pull their own weight. No slackers. Everyone contributes. In the case of Aspiration, everyone had to open up, take in what other people thought, and then hash it all out with no recriminations. Mitch felt as though, in his own corner of the world, he was leading a movement. Finance had never been like this, but he seemed to have gained the confidence of his team. At least, they still gave him the benefit of the doubt – probably because they were making good money.

Mitch learned a lot about leadership, and the role that collaboration plays in success. For example:

- A leader pushes the envelope, and accepts that there may be push-back from his team.

- If a leader comes up with a brave new idea, he'll be frustrated if he doesn't test – just be sure enough so as not to casually put people at risk.
- Collaboration benefits from guardrails – there is no embarrassment in providing off-ramps and brakes.
- If your collaborators see tangible benefits in doing things your way, they will likely stick with you.
- The human element of collaboration is important, even where the collaboration is not primarily about people's personal relationship.

So far, Aspiration is still turning sizable profits. Mitch has ceased, for now, feeling restless. "After all these years," he told me, "I think I've hit my stride." He thinks a good leader doesn't accept limitations until he tries to push past them.

This story concerns a medical center departmental chair who is ambitious for his department. Through a series of staged questions, responses, and offers to the right people, he learns how to draw these people into his department and how to help them become productive. He becomes a more effective, prominent leader – and his department increases in stature.

So, as you read this story, ask yourself:

- *Do I know how to ask questions that will engage people to join in my project?*
- *Do I learn from people's responses sufficiently so that I can tailor my next round of questions?*
- *Can I find people who are close to the people that I want to engage, and who can help me design effective questions?*
- *Do I recognize that questions are often open-ended, and that I am likely to learn what I least expected to learn?*
- *Do I recognize communication as a predicate to designing an effective project, and do I keep the lines open throughout the project?*

The physician/chair in this story learned how to answer these questions affirmatively. He is still learning (which leaders inevitably must do).

Leaders Learn to ask the Right Questions

People Will Fall in Line Behind you When You Know How to Approach Them

Dr. R walked into my office with the journal *JAMA Neurology* under his arm. I can tell a lot about clients from what they're carrying. They're signaling me ("Hey, see this briefcase? I'm just making time for you," or "See these Bergdorf bags? I shop, so deal with it"). It's like they want to get past the preliminaries by cueing me to fix on some crucial aspect of their lives. So, before we even shook hands, I responded on cue, deducing that Dr. R practiced neurology and wouldn't dare miss out on the latest developments. I figured he wanted me to understand that neurology would underline our consultation – even though I was hardly a neurologist.

I was right.

Dr. R was Chair of Neurology at the largest department of any New York City medical center. I knew that department. It offered excellent clinical services, with core strengths in Alzheimer's Disease and progressive dementia, as well as movement disorders, strokes, epilepsy, and headaches. Dr. R's own research into Alzheimer's was world-renowned, and was consistently funded by the NIH. It had earned him the top spot in the department.

So, I wondered out loud why he had come to see me. "You're doing great work," I said, "though I know that's when most problems seem to arise." It was a polite way of suggesting that – like anyone who carried around a name-brand journal – he was afraid of letting anything get past him.

"Yes," he said, "everything's fine. But I feel like the department has plateaued." In other words, like so many high-achievers who consult me (with problems that most other people would envy), he wanted to find – that is, create – the next challenge, and then figure out how to meet it. "You know," he told me, "I identify with the department. I feel responsible for its stature, the way I do for my own." The attitude was admirable, but suggested as well a type of insecurity that (in my psychiatric practice) I could deal with in clinical terms to alleviate the potential for stress. But in the context in which Dr. R. presented, with an emphasis on practical guidance, I thought we might explore some concrete, department-building options.

Dr. R didn't skip a beat. He started at the top. "If I could make the department world class – say, like Langone, Hopkins, the Mayo Clinic – then *I'd* be a world-class." When I suggested that he already was, he countered, "But not *yet* as Chair. I want to cover all the bases."

I knew where this was going. "You don't really have a problem," I said, "so much as you have ambition. But we can work with that."

"How?" he asked, which was a fair question.

The center had an award-winning full-time faculty, dedicated to clinical care, research, and teaching. Facilities were exceptional. Residents clamored for positions. "We offer some of the most sought-after fellowships anywhere," he said, unable to keep from praising the department even while he felt it could do more.

I assumed that he was reaching for something beyond more research, grants, and publications – the bread and butter of academic medical departments. I thought maybe he wanted to add some flair. "Are you thinking," I asked, "about more public engagement? Perhaps a few Sanjay Guptas?" I had been on TV a couple of times, and received positive feedback.

"I hadn't thought of that," he said, "but I'm thinking of something more systemic – something that goes to the heart of how we serve the community."

Okay, outreach of a different kind. I followed up this cue by asking "So, do you have any underutilized resources that you could deploy, that would draw the department closer to the community?"

Dr. R had held his position for four years, and by now had taken stock of every weak link. "Well," he said, "I guess the voluntary faculty is underutilized. They teach, and are especially good with the residents, but they're not offering care – they're not even participating in clinical trials." So, here was an opening.

Apparently, the department had over 600 voluntary faculty. "I've never approached them on what they might do," he said. "I should, since they all have service requirements." So, Dr. R was *himself* underutilized – he could have, but hadn't called on this cohort which he had allowed to drift. "Why not invite them to talk with you," I asked, "I'm sure they'll have productive ideas." After all, he was offering them a chance to practice the best medicine (they just had to figure out how that would work given their existing practices). My point was that you can open an inquiry without defining all the terms in advance. Just specify the general direction, and let other people help define where you're headed – together.

I asked whether there was someone among the voluntary faculty whom he might initially consult, perhaps to get a sense of how best to approach the others. "Maybe they could even help you lead the project," I suggested, "since they would be closer to the voluntary faculty and appreciate their perspective." Dr. R said he had just the person in mind, a certain Dr. A whom he met with regularly anyway and whom the residents adored. "He's a great teacher," he said, "and he brings in private funding. He's expressed an interest in doing more." So, we thought about how this collaboration could work.

"It's probably best," I said, "to find out what he already knows about the voluntary faculty – what would they like to do at the center, provided they were offered the opportunity? But be prepared to learn stuff that you hadn't anticipated." That is, when you ask questions for the first time, you should be ready for responses you hadn't anticipated. A leader learns how to adjust, and to move ahead accordingly.

I also suggested that once there was a comprehensive list, he and Dr. A could determine (given the available facilities, existing openings, and each person's practice and expertise) what it was possible to offer. "Maybe some options will suit some voluntary faculty better than others – you'll want to tailor your offerings to each individual." It would require evaluating 600 practitioners closely, but it would forestall the risk of a general offering that might not work for everyone. "Part of leading a project like this," I said, "is not alienating people in the process. People should feel comfortable, and like you're talking to them."

So, part of communication in a setting where you're not sure how people will respond is to ensure that however they respond will be within the range of the possible. You don't know just what they will say, and you want to provide them leeway, but you should protect yourself by protecting them from choices that aren't practicable.

After a couple of months, Dr. R and Dr. A had worked out a list of what voluntary faculty might do. In addition to more teaching and supervision, they could help secure grants and participate in clinical trials. They could help recruit people for such trials among their own patients. They could help to develop and administer more fellowships. They could even help in communicating with other voluntary faculty, and draw up reports that Dr. R could use in making follow-up contacts.

I pointed out that, at least in its initial phases, communication need not operate on a one-on-one basis. "You can deputize people to do some of the work. You deputized Dr. A, and you can draw on other voluntary faculty once they learn what you're looking for." In effect, leadership requires drawing people into your orbit. As they populate your universe, they become helpful. Here, they will ask the questions and gain the information that Dr. R can then put to work.

There is also an element of uncertainty. He didn't know what information – what options – he and Dr. A would initially consider, but he was able to use the results to design a list of options that he could tailor to each member of the voluntary faculty. "I guess," he later told me, "it comes down to knowing whom to ask; when to ask; and finally what to ask based on consideration of whom I need to ask." Communication can occur in stages. Leaders are there at each stage to interpret it, apply it, and move on.

Dr. R told me that many of the options that he offered to voluntary faculty were possibilities that he might have guessed. "But until I went through the process of vetting those possibilities," he said, "I didn't know if they were realistic and for whom they were realistic." He also acknowledged, somewhat sheepishly, that Dr. A had been right there all along – "right under my nose" – and that he had never thought to recruit him to assay the voluntary faculty. "He became the fulcrum of my initiative. I couldn't have embarked on this project but for him."

Of course, Dr. R's efforts to raise the department's profile has not gone unnoticed by other departments in the center. "They see more voluntary faculty taking part in what we do – even organizing conferences, with a lot of exposure. They want to know how I did it." He tells them that it's a question of targeted outreach, of knowing whom to ask, what to ask, and when. "It's got to be based on the internal configuration of each department, and what it needs. If they can figure that out, they should be able to figure out the rest.

As Dr. R pursued (and is still pursuing) his project, here is some of what he learned (and is learning):

- Leaders do not need to communicate with everyone all at once in order to obtain useful information – they can communicate in stages, and apply what they've learned to any communication that follows.
- Leaders find experts who are close to the people that interest them, and who can help design the best ways of approaching them

- It's important to know whom to ask; what to ask; and when to ask it, not only to get the best information, but so as not to make anyone uncomfortable by offering options to which they are not suited
- Sometimes, people are just waiting to be asked. They may be right under our noses, or just preoccupied – but they will step right up if we approach them in ways that they find attractive, and likely to benefit them.

Dr. R made several useful connections during a staged process of asking questions. He pushed himself to think creatively at each stage. "As a leader," he told me, "I learned how to approach people that I had barely known. "What broke the ice," he said, "was asking the right questions."

***

These stories demonstrate how communication and collaboration work *in practice*. They are not merely theoretical ("Always leave the channels of communication open," or "Think before you explain"). Thus, the stories illustrate people back-tracking and making up for mistakes. The stories shows them changing course and revising their message. That's how real communication works, and that's how effective communication lasts. Some useful take-aways from this chapter include:

- An effective communicator acts strategically, mapping out how his or her statement will affect people, and create interest in their joining a project.
- Communication can give rise to collaboration, and continues into any collaboration.
- Start from the assumption that what you have to say is interesting – if you cannot project your own enthusiasm, others will not respond.
- Not everyone has to agree on everything to become your collaborator – the point is to keep up the communication so that people can still work together towards the main objective.
- Effective communication and collaboration produce synergy, which multiplies your effectiveness even if your resources are minimal.

The people in these stories are not experts, but are open to learning at every turn. Communication and collaboration are two-way streets. It's crucial to remain open to what you can learn – you're never just issuing directives.

Reference

Fisher, Roger and William Ury, *Getting to Yes: Negotiating Agreement Without Giving In* (New York: Penguin), 2011.

Chapter V

Responsibility

When leaders assume "responsibility," they take ownership of a situation, managing it in as many dimensions as necessary so that problems are resolved and all the moving parts operate in sync. They may need to call on skills they didn't know they had – or develop new ones fast. But beyond skills, responsibility is an attitude. It implies attentiveness, and the will to make hard choices. It means that you can take the heat and stand up for what you think is right. Ultimately, it means that you don't just think inside whatever box you're in. You take prudent risks; you exercise imagination; you don't stop trying until the change that needs to happen happens.

Of course, everyone makes mistakes. Leaders sometimes make the mistake of thinking they're not supposed to make mistakes (or, at least, not to seem as though they have). So, they fudge and backtrack. They deflect blame and offer excuses. But responsible leaders acknowledge mistakes and set about fixing them. In this sense, they take the long view. They understand that, down the road, people will respect their transparency and appreciate the proactive effort that – ideally – made things right (or, at least, better). So, assuming responsibility can determine how people ultimately regard a leader.

Think of responsibility as testing your mettle in public. Have you shown yourself to be honest? Are you strong, and strategic enough to get out in front of situations before the fallout overtakes the whole enterprise? These are crucial questions, if only because trust is crucial to a leader's continuing success.

But responsibility also refers to looking after a project or an enterprise so that it continually responds to new demands, and everyone involved remains employed, satisfied, and high-functioning. It requires clearing away obstacles, as well as mentoring the next generation of vital employees. So, responsibility requires cultivating what might be considered old-fashioned virtues, notwithstanding the trend towards leaders who view themselves as hired problem-solvers, who never fully commit themselves long-term.

The stories in this chapter illustrate how everyday leaders recover from their mistakes, or take on new responsibilities, or stand up for ethical imperatives. They see problems in their own lives, and decide to address them on a larger

DOI: 10.4324/9781003437635-6

scale. They forget about their comfort zones. These leaders are complicated, sometimes fighting rearguard actions against their own regrets or limitations (it's rare for a leader to separate themselves entirely from their personality – but they can work on renovations).

Of course, a leader's ultimate responsibility is to ensure a seamless transition to the next generation of leadership. Here too, they must step outside their comfort zone, since who likes planning their own departure? Who likes admitting that the company they built may look and feel different? The final story in this chapter addresses this challenge. Particularly, it takes up the importance of mentorship, as the prior leader grooms the new one while resisting the urge to be possessive.

In assuming responsibility, the leaders in these stories figure out how to create change and manage it effectively. They show resilience (a huge component of taking on responsibility over the long haul). They exercise imagination. Take-aways from these stories include:

- Taking on responsibility can be a form of damage control, reflecting on the leader's skills, tolerance for risk, and commitment.
- The responsible leader is always thinking ahead, even while he or she may be swamped by immediate concerns.
- Taking responsibility reflects a willingness to change one's outlook, habits, and ways of relating to other people – it means getting out of your comfort zone.
- If love means never having to say you're sorry, then responsibility is just the opposite – leaders show their human side, and respect other people's humanity.
- By taking responsibility, leaders discern problems and determine how to fix them – they commit resources strategically.

None of this comes easily. But the responsible leader is a good strategist. He or she figures out how to get from A to B and beyond by well-coordinated steps that add up to good strategy.

In this story, a physician loses his job due to a professional mistake. But does he give up? No! He acknowledges his mistake, and uses it to define a new leadership position: advising other physicians on how to avoid the same mistake. He literally creates a sub-field within his own field of pain management, in which he demonstrates – based on his own experience – how to avoid the same pitfalls. He also leads an advocacy group that develops and promotes policies based on what he has learned.

So, as you read this story, ask yourself:

- *Am I willing to own my mistakes and learn from them, or do I try to bury them so that no will find out what I did (almost always a losing strategy)?*

- *Am I able to leverage my mistakes, turning them into assets that bolster my credibility when I talk about my profession?*
- *When I accept responsibility, do I define my mistakes, or do I let other people define them?*
- *Do I understand the level of care expected of me, or do I allow my zeal (to help, to hit a target, to beat my competitors) deflect me from exercising sufficient care?*

The physician in this story struggled with these questions but, finally, he found the right answers. Taking responsibility for our mistakes is never easy. But it provides a surprising path towards becoming a leader and sustaining the credibility of one's leadership.

Leaders Take Responsibility for their Mistakes

The Best Leaders Turn Their Mistakes into Opportunities

Dr. L is a leading advocate for "defensive medicine" – the protocols by which physicians reduce their own risks when prescribing drugs that patients can abuse. But he found his calling the hard way. Earlier in his career, he needed such advice himself. His evolution, as a practitioner and advocate, illustrates how taking responsibility for your mistakes can propel you towards leadership, and will underscore the credibility of your initiatives.

I counseled Dr. L during his necessary, sometimes painful evolution. When he finally emerged, I was inspired to explore resilience on a professional level (I've since written several papers on the subject). In terms of leadership, I wanted to understand how bouncing back from mistakes helps us help others with ethical and practical dilemmas that surface throughout a professional lifetime. In this sense, Dr. L's story is intrinsic to mine. Together, they create a feedback loop that shouts, "We learn from each other, even when we're not trying to!"

When Dr. L first came to see me, he declared "I'm a walking irony, a pain management doctor who can't manage his pain." Clients who put a spin on themselves before even shaking my hand, want me to see them through their own eyes. Dr. L, apparently, was presenting himself as incompetent, unable to apply his professional skills to fix what ailed him.

But not so fast. "We're talking about different kinds of pain, aren't we?" I asked. "You're not here for anything physiological." He conceded the point, although I still got his message: Dr. L saw himself as behind an 8-ball. He wanted help in pushing it out of the way.

So, once we had properly introduced ourselves, I asked what was going on.

"I'm in trouble," he said. "I had to leave my high-profile practice for one in the professional boonies – and everyone knows why." In other words, he'd been professionally humiliated. He needed some roadmap for a comeback.

I needed some background. The pain management practice he'd left had been in a major hospital. Highly trained physicians prescribed opioids and other controlled substances. He'd helped hundreds of patients over the years, taking account of their different tolerances for pain, their physiology, genetic background, and even their culture ("Latino men," he told me "never complain until the pain almost floors them – they're terrified of seeming weak").

I thought the glib stereotyping was the result of agitation, preventing him from maintaining a proper, unbiased scientific demeanor. But rather than call him on it, I just asked that he explain what had happened.

I got the whole work-up.

About 18 months earlier, a patient had complained of terrible non-specific pain that had left him disabled and unemployed. He had been referred by another physician, who had diagnosed fibromyalgia but had treated him unsuccessfully. "When the guy walked into my office," Dr. L said, "he looked like a wreck." But rather than just switch medications, Dr. L thought that the same prescription, plus exercise and a high-protein diet, might help.

After a month, however, it had not. So, Dr. L increased the dosage, although still within the therapeutic limit. "Different dosages can cause different outcomes," he told me. "So, I wasn't worried – people vary in how they respond." As a psychiatrist who prescribes an array of mood-altering drugs, I agreed. But I also realized that upping someone's dosage within acceptable limits could not, itself, have caused the major problem that Dr. L described.

"There's more," I said flatly. Dr. L said there was.

But what? After a few months on the new dosage, the patient had apparently improved. In fact, he was even looking for a job. "So, for a while, I felt good about myself," Dr. L told me. "It felt even better when this patient sent me other patients – we started a support group, and everyone was great about showing up."

That is, until six federal agents also showed up, and hauled Dr. L off in handcuffs. A photo of the arrest leaked to the tabloids, whose headlines screamed "Gotcha!" One front-page story declared "Fancy pain management doc busted in drug conspiracy." It turned out that the original patient, as well as the rest of the support group, had been selling some of their meds on the street. When they got caught, they named Dr. L as a co-conspirator. As Dr. L described it to me, "They told the police I never asked questions. They interpreted that as a wink and a nod. They said I acquiesced."

It sounded like a late-night TV crime show, where some clueless dupe takes the fall in a low-life plot to save a few street hoods. In this reality knock-off, maybe the police didn't understand the complexities of prescribing controlled substances. In Dr. L's view, they just saw him as an easy mark. "Hey, forget that I went to medical school," he told me, "they wanted to make their quota." But whatever their socio-cultural motivations, they clearly disdained Dr. L's liberal prescribing practices, which undermined their objective to get these drugs off the street. "I guess they thought," he said, "that those guys couldn't have scored but for my intervention. So, of course, I'm guilty."

Eventually, the legal process allowed Dr. L to retain his license ("Maybe the judge watches crime shows," he joked. "The good guys always get off in the end"). I thought it was funny that we both saw the TV angle – though he saw it as more favorable to himself. But in any case, the judge recognized that Dr. L had been well-intentioned. "It's what saved me," he said. But that didn't save his practice at the hospital. He was let go on account of the negative exposure. "They said *they* had to recover from the publicity, even more than I did," he said. "Okay, I get that." But he still wanted to work in the profession.

That's when he came to see me about how to resume his career – that is, how to recover from an apparent display of bad judgment that had knocked him sideways.

We began by discussing necessary first steps. I said how important it was to be transparent with any new group that he interviewed. "It's all in the public record," I told him, "so you can't hide it. But you can also explain how it happened."

"Well, how *did* it happen?" he asked. He meant that his responsibility was murky. That is, what could he be transparent *about*? He hadn't sold the drugs. He had, in the eyes of the law, made it easier for would-be criminals to sell them, though he hadn't realized that *that* would be the result. So, in effect, he bore indirect responsibility, based on his failure to adequately assess the claims and intentions of his patients.

We batted these ideas around for a while. Finally, he asked, "Do I say that I wanted to help, and didn't pay attention to the kind of people I was helping?" I said that was a start. The point was to take responsibility for what he had done, but in a way that does not allow someone else to define it – neither the police (who did not understand the complexities) or the tabloids (which only want to attract readers). "You should demonstrate that you own you own your mistakes," I said, "but you should be clear as to what mistakes you have actually made."

Based on this nuanced approach, Dr. L began what he called his Responsibility Offensive. "I'm going to tell my story," he said, "so that other doctors can learn how not to lapse into inattention." This was part of his larger campaign to get hired again, bolstered by his status as a leader in pain management who had something to teach his peers.

He gave talks about assessing patients before taking them on – are they hypochondriacs, malingerers, drug-seeking layabouts, or (as in his case) are they willing to abuse the system to make a fast buck? He spoke at pain management conferences, and turned his talks into articles that appeared in prominent journals. His evidence was empirical, that is, based in his own experience. "I owned my experience," he said, "and that gave what I said credibility." It also gave him confidence – he wouldn't be caught off guard by someone who'd read the tabloids and threw all that stuff back at him. "I've outed myself," he said.

As a been-there-done-that veteran, he could provide clear-eyed, explicit instructions. It was never enough just to want to help people manage their pain. "You should ask about their history with drugs and prior involvement with the legal system. Look them up on major social media platforms – you'd be amazed what people come right out and admit." I thought this was prudent advice. "But what makes me a draw," he said, "is that I lived everything I have to say. I wouldn't be a draw if I hadn't accepted my role in what happened." He could have tried to explain it away ("Those police are so simple-minded," "The tabloids blow up everything"). But instead, he leveraged it. That was key.

In a few months, he was hired by a smaller practice that liked his emerging leadership role in an area of pain management that had not received the attention that it should. "I have a supervisor now, who vets my choice of patients before I can take them on," he told me. "But I expected that – I think it's provisional." His goal is to establish himself as *the* advocate for defensive medicine in the practice of pain management. "Unlike most other doctors," he said, "we see patients who *seek* drugs – heavy doses on a long-term basis. How do you keep from experiencing what I did?"

Once he got his footing in the new practice, he started a nonprofit organization, Focus on Prescription Drugs, that would advocate at federal and state levels to develop and advance policies to mitigate the risk of prescription drug abuse while allowing for appropriate, medically supervised treatment of issues relating to debilitating pain. Among its recommendations were:

- States should incorporate physician input into pain management laws and regulations.
- States should implement prescription drug monitoring programs and be able to share registry information.
- Continuing medical education (CME) programs should include instruction on how physicians can guard against the risk of prescription drug abuse – for example, by assessing patients' legal backgrounds.
- Increase federal support for research into optimal pain management strategies that include alternatives not reliant on prescription drugs.
- Law enforcement agencies should recognize that doctors who prescribe prescription drugs are not instrumental to their abuse provided they take reasonable precautions to prevent abuse.

The organization is also battling high prescription drug costs, which make them attractive to sell on the street at a discount.

So far, Dr. L has signed up hundreds of pain management doctors and, he boasts, "I'm just getting started. But, of course, the main point is that because he decided to own his mistakes, he is now able to lead from a perspective of real, personal experience with the issues he addresses. His credibility is undoubted.

During our discussions, he emerged into leadership from a place of significant professional humiliation. But rather than just discard that humiliation, he turned it to his advantage ("I lived through this. You can trust me"). As a result, he learned important lessons concerning leadership:

- Don't hide from your mistakes. Learn from them, and make them work from you.
- Be transparent about your mistakes, especially if people can readily find out about them – you don't want to seem like a liar, or like someone who doesn't take his mistakes seriously.
- A leader gains credibility by taking responsibility for everything he or she has done – the successes as well as the failures.
- When you accept responsibility for mistakes, you should define those mistakes – don't let someone else define them for you.
- Taking responsibility for your mistakes is a form of protection – nobody can catch you off guard.
- If you want to lead with confidence, you should be honest about yourself.

Dr. L carefully applied these principles (though first he had to learn them). They became the basis of a leadership position in his field. But the sciences (including the medical science) are no different from other fields in this respect. Well, perhaps the sciences are more intellectually demanding, and the chance to slip up is commensurately greater. But still, anyone can make a mistake. The point is to own that mistake, and turn it to your advantage.

This story involves a financial advisor whose son has autism. Based on her professional skills and personal experience, she assumes a leadership role in advising families faced with the challenge of caring for autistic children long-term. She assumes responsibility by recognizing an unmet need and figuring out – step by step – how meet it.

So, as you read this story, ask yourself:

- *Am I alert to the needs of people who could benefit from my professional skills and personal experience?*
- *Am I willing to assume responsibility for meeting those needs?*
- *Do I cultivate empathy as a basis for assuming responsibility?*
- *Do I recognize how my personal experience complements my professional skills, so that I can design practical – but also empathic – approaches to persistent needs?*
- *Do I make long-term commitments that may require me to reconfigure my other commitments?*

The woman in this story learned that she could answer these questions in the affirmative. She put that knowledge of herself to practical use, assuming responsibility for initiatives that benefited thousands of people.

Responsibility Emerges with the Need

Leaders Apply Their Professional Skills and Personal Experience

People consult me at inflection points. They know that what they do – and who they are – must change. But they aren't sure how change will occur, and where they will end up once it does. Will it happen all at once, the result of some exigency that sweeps them along? Or will it evolve, allowing them time to think, and adapt along the way? They wonder what new responsibilities will descend on them, and whether they'll even recognize themselves once everything shakes out. "I'm getting to know myself all over again," one client told me. Change, when it comes, can be multi-dimensional and daunting.

When Christina arrived in my office, she saw change coming. "I'm going through a rough patch," she said. "I need to find a new direction."

As with many clients, I thought about suggesting my psychiatric practice to allay such anxiety. But instead, I listened. Christina's demeanor was commanding, and I assumed that however anxious she was, she would handle it. Her real concern, she told me, was to see her way past what she called her recent "shock."

Now in her late forties, Christina was a successful financial consultant, with a specialty in helping women manage post-divorce. In the international circles where she was a fixture, demand for her services was booming. She and her husband, also in finance, led a stylish, One-Percenter life ("We own a share in a private jet, and it's *so* useful"). But the hitch came when, past forty, she found herself pregnant – after ten years and three other kids. "We never thought of not having Danny," she told me. "I figured I'd take time off, and then life would snap back to normal." Except it didn't.

Starting at around three months, just when Christina had hired a nanny and was set to resume her practice, Danny's developmental problems became unmistakable. "I knew how kids should act," she told me, "I've been around the block a few times." Danny didn't babble or respond to voices. He didn't grab for Christina's keys, when she dangled them. He displayed an odd incuriosity, even about his body ("My other kids investigated their toes," she said, "and were fascinated by what fingers could do. But Danny just flailed around when he wasn't lying there inert"). His motor skills were minimal. He didn't crawl. His pediatrician asked for detailed weekly updates. Though Christina tried to allow for what she hoped was mere slowness ("People told me that Einstein didn't talk until three"), there was no denying that Danny wasn't making *any* progress.

Finally, Christina brought Danny for tests at the Yale school of medicine, where a clinic specialized in children's developmental disorders. "They diagnosed ASD," she told me – autism spectrum disorder. About one in 36 kids receives that diagnosis, and boys are four times more likely to receive it than girls. From an epidemiological perspective, these diagnoses are increasing, possibly due to environmental factors and the desire to get kids into treatment. There is a "spectrum" because autism is a multi-system form of mental and developmental retardation affecting cognitive, social, sensory-processing, and physical functioning. It's every parent's nightmare.

"I was devastated," Christina told me. "As parents, John and I fell into the typical pattern – first we were in denial, then we blamed ourselves." It was understandable. According to the literature (which Christina had mastered by the time she came to see me), genetic factors are estimated to contribute 40 to 80% of ASD risk. Gene variants, combined with environmental factors, parental age, birth complications, as well as factors that have not been identified, determine the degree of risk. "I couldn't forgive myself – why, when I was past forty, did I go ahead with this birth? And by the way, it wasn't easy." Whether or not I was conscious of it, I flipped into psychiatrist mode. "You can't blame yourself," I said. "It's happening to all kinds of people." She knew that, of course, but still it was hard to accept.

By the time Christina came to see me, Danny was six. "We started him in treatment right away," she told me. "But we've yet to see significant progress." Some kids respond to medication and therapy better than others. At six, Danny could say a few words, but he never made eye contact. He'd have a thought but, when he couldn't express it, he became aggressive and need to be restrained. He never ate with the family because he would throw food. When he wasn't entirely withdrawn, he would scream. "Sometimes, I thought he smiled at me," Christina told me, "but his doctors said that was facial contortion." The possibility of mainstreaming him in school was vanishingly small.

Recently, Danny had begun tapping at pictures on a keyboard. His attention span was slightly improved. "He likes how the pictures pop up on the screen. It's like he knows he caused something," she said. The trouble was that while he could minimally relate to a virtual world, it was still remote from his natural environment. Nonetheless, there was hope that if his attention span continued to improve, he might learn letters and finally tap out words. Real speech – of some sort – was the goal, but it could take years of practice, therapy, and advances in treatment modalities.

So, how was I supposed to help? Of all the clients I had counseled, Christina pulled at my heart more than any. I have three great kids. I could only imagine how she felt. I hoped she didn't look at family pictures around my office – would she feel somehow resentful, or like a failure? But that was my psychiatrist head, generating awkward possibilities. In fact, I knew that Christina had not come to me for moral support, much less advice on how to handle Danny. She had the best advice in the world, although she chafed at Danny's lumbering progress. What she wanted, as she announced right up front, was some new "direction" for her life, where Danny's condition would be an integral part of it.

"What," I asked, "would you do if you could do anything right now?"

Christina was still counseling women, but she had cut back to 20 hours a week. The rest of her time was devoted to caring for Danny, following his treatment, participating in support groups, and reading the literature. "I must have read every study in English, French, and Chinese," she told me (Christina had studied in China after college, and read the language proficiently). Still, I knew she wanted more. She had a keen intelligence, and was a problem-solver. "The women I help," she told me, "are earning two and three times what their exes gave them." I thought once she settled on a new direction, she could have that same multiplier effect.

We kept talking. Christina knew that Danny would be central to her life for the rest of her life. "John and I are putting money aside," she told me, "so when we're too old to care for Danny, he can access the care that he needs. Maybe he'll be an outpatient, maybe he'll need some group setting where he'll live full-time." I imagined Danny in a facility just when Christina and John were as well. In this sense, autism inverts the usual configuration of parent/child care-giving: the child remains a burden, never able to care for aging parents.

Autism elevates parental responsibility, not just when a child is young, but permanently. Christina was coming to terms with this reality. Luckily, she had the financial resources to provide for Danny if, presumably, he could never live independently.

The situation got me thinking. "Suppose," I asked, "you could bootstrap your plans for Danny's future into a new career model. You could counsel other families with kids that have mental health issues." It seemed almost obvious. Christina had achieved stunning success as a financial strategist, and now she lived and breathed the challenges of autism. So, why not put the two together, and help other families to finance life with an autistic child? She knew that caring for such a child affected every member of a family. Everyone helped however they could. Her own children constantly offered support. "The whole family takes responsibility for him. Now and for the foreseeable future." What if she could project that sense of responsibility into a larger space, where many families could benefit from her expertise?

Christina jumped on the idea. She knew she had to pivot towards a more engaged, autism-focused career, and this seemed the way to go. "After all," I asked, "how many financial advisors understand the demands on families that autism presents? You could become a leader in the field." It was an emerging field. As diagnoses of autism increased, so would the need for experts to help people cope. Christina's combination of financial and personal experience positioned her to assume responsibility regarding an expanding cohort that she could benefit.

As we spoke, the idea began to make sense – not just to me, but to Christina. She could see herself as leading a vitally necessary movement, helping families to face the lengthening needs of autistic children. "Years ago," she told me, "I realized that women needed financial guidance post-divorce. I helped create a niche among financial advisors that focused on their situation – maybe I can do the same now."

Leaders recognize a need and then fill it. They take responsibility for a problem and help solve it. Christina was perfectly positioned to do so. It would mean enlarging her intra-family responsibility (which only involved Danny), and applying it in a greater social space. It would mean empathizing with these other affected people – seeing their need in terms aligned with her own. Her ability to recognize the problem reflects her understanding of (and caring about) the same problem among so many families.

So, Christina went for it. "I had always been active in my support groups," she told me, "but now I assumed a leadership role. I promoted financial planning based on a long-term commitment to an autistic child." Christina was swamped with inquiries. She had touched a nerve. People sought consultations. They told friends in other groups. They suggested she write a regular newsletter. "I hadn't expected this kind of response," she said, "but it was gratifying. In not too long, national groups – ranging from those dedicated to autism, to ones involved with finances and social work among the disabled – all wanted interviews. "Single mothers are particularly interested," she told me. "It's hard enough coping right now, let alone putting aside funds for the future." She felt that it was all becoming bigger than her own financial practice. It seemed like the response was only going to grow.

Christina had become everyone's go-to expert in what she now called "integrative finance for families dealing with ASD." Of course, she worried that her message was a downer – who likes the prospect of an infinite burden? – but she emphasized that with careful planning, people could get ahead of the financial burden and, in that sense, minimize it. "I said it was no different from retirement planning – in both cases, we should put enough by to last as long the funds are needed, and to meet the unexpected."

I asked whether she had made a sufficient pivot, or whether all this interest in her work entailed other possibilities. "You know," I said, "there is probably a lot more you could do, provided your family is on board."

She said she'd think about it.

When we met a couple of weeks later, she had. "John and I sold our share in the Learjet," she told me. "We're endowing a nonprofit." Given that a one-eighth share in a midsize private jet sells for around $800,000, that was a major commitment ("We don't fly much anyway," she laughed, "so we may as well put that jet to *some* use"). I asked how the nonprofit was related to the "other possibilities" we had discussed.

She told me that "We're calling it Danny's Place. It's a clearinghouse for everything affecting how you deal with ASD long-term. Particularly, it will connect people to financial resources they can use in arranging local, long-term care." The up-front funding would permit her to hire researchers and consultants. "Ultimately," she said, "we'll get grants – once we establish a track record. I want the Place to be self-sustaining." She was thinking long-term, as she always did.

Christina said she would spend half her available time in her own practice, and the other half ensuring that Danny's Place succeeded. "I don't see either activity as competing with the other," she said. "My practice is high-end, while the Place offers people a DIY option that, in most cases, is sufficient." Christina was always the canny businesswoman.

But more to the point, she had constructed a new, comprehensive long-term advising environment in which she was the intellectual/emotional leader. It had grown out of her personal experience, but it was designed to reach thousands – maybe millions – of families facing what hers now faced. She saw a need, addressed it, and then addressed it again in a way that could serve even more people. She took responsibility at every stage as the project evolved. During her journey, she learned that:

- Empathy can serve as the basis for a type of targeted leadership where you take responsibility for what you understand – and, in fact, have personally experienced.
- Responsibility consists in recognizing a need and then meeting it (as Christina would say, long-term and in perpetuity).
- Responsible leaders are generous.
- You never know when you need to step up as a leader, and you never know how gratifying the response may be.
- Taking responsibility can grow into a calling.

Christina never expected how radically her life would change. But Danny's birth changed everything. By taking responsibility for what she saw as a large and growing need – that is, by applying her unique set of skills and experience – she became a leader in a space that she effectively defined.

This story concerns the principal and founder of a hedge fund, who assumes the responsibility for saving it when the pandemic threatens its profitability. He stops thinking like a geek, and learns to bolster relationships among his investors and staff. In effect, he learns how to change the firm's culture by changing the way he thinks.

So, as you read this story, ask yourself:

- *Am I able to accept new ways of thinking, even if they pull me out of my comfort zone?*
- *Do I recognize that what works in one context may not work at all in another?*
- *Do I have a handle on the prevailing culture of the organization that I lead, and can I assume responsibility for changing it?*
- *Am I capable of publicizing my organization's internal changes, so that people external to it become aware of them and react sympathetically?*

The leader in this story was finally able to answer these questions in the affirmative. But it was not easy. He had to seriously reassess his modus operandi. He put his ego on the line. Eventually, he did so well that other organizations adopted the changes that he made.

Leaders take Responsibility for the Culture of a Business

Changing a Business' Culture May Be the Way to Save It

Jack is the founder and principal of a hedge fund with $5 billion under management. On Wall Street that would not normally take your breath away – hedge funds with twenty times that invested are considered "middle-range." But what sets Jack apart is the lore surrounding him. Unlike most of his peers, who came up through the gilded purlieus of Harvard and Wharton, Jack emerged out of the comparative wilderness. He never even went to business school. His father drove a cab. He had majored in math at a local college, found his calling as a "quant," and in three or four years was universally regarded as a genius. Jack just thought he was having fun.

But when people consult me, it's because the fun has stopped.

"So, what's up?" I asked, trying to keep the conversation from a nose-dive into angst before we even said hello. I'd read about Jack's troubles in the *Wall Street Journal*, which covered him from a breathless, contradictory perspective of told-you-so and disbelief. Apparently, he perplexed the reporters as much as he now seemed to worry himself.

I asked Jack to give me some history. "Tell me in your own words," I said. "I don't consider the *Journal* the last word on any of this."

Jack, now in his mid-thirties started with a virtual day-by-day account of his career. The guy was a total geek. "Wait," I said. "I'm not the SEC – just give me an outline, not every detail." I realized that outside the realm of numbers, Jack was uncomfortable. This was my first clue as to what might have gone wrong at his fund. Maybe he'd had trouble with his staff, or even with investors. While all these people cared about numbers and the fund's monthly returns, they still needed a degree of cosseting, if only to feel valued by the reining genius calling the shots.

"Look," I said. "Just tell me how you got to this point. What brings you here *now*?"

I got the 50-cent history. In his late twenties, Jack had capitalized on his reputation (as he did on everything). He broke away from the pack, started his own fund, and was headed for the stratosphere . . . until now, when he has almost crashed and burned. It seemed prescient, in a sad, ironic way, that he had named the fund Comet Investments – a flashy phenomenon that streaks across the sky, then disappears into interstellar space. Jack didn't seem the type to appreciate the irony.

As he filled me in, Jack said the firm made consistent gains over seven or eight years. "We had a 2 and 20 model and averaged over 10% a year," he said, "so you can do the math." Could I? Well, considering what came next, it didn't really matter.

In early 2020, the pandemic upended everything.

Comet had taken a large position in the airline industry and, when that shut down, the firm suffered its first losing year. Jack told me "There was nothing really to hedge it against since the whole sector was collapsing." Comet tried to refocus its investments towards online gaming and telecoms, but these positions didn't initially gain much traction either. So, 2021 was another losing year.

Some investors pulled their capital. A few portfolio managers quit. A week later, Jack was in my office.

"Well," he said, "You can't fix my investment strategy, but – short of that – can you help me restore confidence among my investors and employees?" He feared that a vicious cycle of financial loss, investor disaffection, and staff departures would put Comet out of business before the pandemic passed and market dynamics returned to some sort of normal. In a way, I thought, he was asking how he could reach out and grab people, retain their commitment . . . and maybe even resuscitate their belief in him as a super-quant Master of the Universe.

"It comes down to communication," I said. "You have to make that your full-time responsibility." I thought he should reinvent the culture at Comet, so that his people projected confidence and investors caught the bug. "You're not just picking winners now," I told him. "You're leading an organization and trying to hold onto clients." It would be an exercise in maturation – for Jack and for Comet. He had to build up relationships within the firm (how else would people be convinced to stay around?), and externally (unless investors believed in Jack, they would take their money elsewhere).

So, we began talking about how he could assume this "responsibility." Jack had never thought about directing the firm's culture, let alone redirecting it, let alone ensuring that it be a vehicle for the firm's salvation. He would just sit with the other quants, decide where to place their (very educated) bets, and then let his managers work out details with investors. The secret ingredient in this black-box hands-off movement of funds was Jack's own charisma. He did not have to say much to anyone. "I largely communicate through the bottom line," he told me. I told him that should stop. If it did not, Comet could flame out.

"Let's start with the investors," I said (I saw them as more likely to leave than his employees, since finding a job would be harder than finding another fund). "You might consider making Comet investor-centric, where each investor feels a personal relationship with you – no more remote, here's-the-deal *fait accompli*." From now on, he decided he would allow investors into the firm's thinking – how does it address the market, and position itself on a daily basis? "You're creating a culture of openness," I said, "where there are no seams. There is a *flow* of data outwards, so that investors feel like part of the enterprise."

This sort of approach – where he and the investors were on the same page – was new to Jack. I watched as he tried to process it. He was used to issuing obiter dicta, so this probably struck him as a come-down, a request to be fully transparent to investors, when he was so much smarter than they were. I wanted to soften his resistance.

"Part of taking responsibility," I said, "is to be responsible to others. This may involve acting outside your comfort zone. Sometimes that means reimagining a firm's culture, and forgoing how you've run things before." He acknowledged that this made sense, though he couldn't help displaying a boyish, bruised-ego grin. "Leaders show flexibility and adaptability, even break their own habits," I commented, "if that's what it takes to change the culture around them." He said he'd have stuff to report when he returned in two weeks.

When Jack came back, he laid out the new "Comet Investor Relations Plan" (which he'd invited *Journal* reporters to cover). Previously, investors received a quarterly report in the mail. "It was old by time it arrived," he told me. "I'm not sure they even read it." This new plan, however, included a bi-weekly report *plus* an online platform where investors could follow Comet's investment positions in real time. "They can watch us think," he said. "It's like watching the Dow Jones Index, only focused on our own selected equities." The platform also included signed commentary on the day's moves, so that investors knew why Comet was making them.

It was terrific. Jack was treating investors as intelligent, engaged, and, most of all, concerned with how Comet was deploying their funds. This was a culture-shift, a break with the paradigm – and Jack was owning it, taking responsibility for it (in effect, in real time). "This may look like a lot more work," I said, "but don't you think investors know that? They realize you've changed your M.O. to make them more comfortable with your operations." Leaders take responsibility – and display it, reimagining how their organization must change on behalf of the people it serves.

Because Jack identified so personally with Comet, he had to change as well. He had to think of himself as responsible not just for its investment strategy but for creating a culture that helped retain investors. "I guess I'm branching out," he said, by which he meant that he was *reaching* out, consistent with his new sense of acting responsively/responsibly.

After we spoke further, Jack arranged a Zoom meeting with each investor, and discussed their individual concerns. "I want them to understand that I'm serious about profits, even in this challenging environment." He told me they must have been reassured, since most of them stayed on. I complimented him on focusing on the relationship rather than simply the bottom line.

Then Jack turned towards reassuring his partners and key personnel. "I had to acknowledge that there would be no bonuses for a while. But I also added that I'd be giving them more say in the decision making." Up until then, he had been the ultimate decision-maker. "I think that part of taking responsibility," he said, "is sharing responsibility. It's empowering people, and will benefit us all." He was planning a series of meeting where everyone would share their expertise and express their views. "I'm going to listen," he said. "We're all going to listen to each other." The point was to make his personnel feel part of Comet. "We're building it back together," he observed.

The idea of distributed responsibility was part of the internal culture-shift that we had discussed. "I want the investors to know that we're changing from the inside out," he said. Nothing is just for show – that new platform only makes sense if it reflects a renovated mode of decision-making." What he meant is that if investors could watch the effect of Comet's deliberations in real time, then those deliberations should reflect an enhanced deliberative process. "I'm putting out a press release on the changes we're making. We're probably on course to change the industry once they see our profits go up (okay, if they do!)"

I was impressed at how quickly Jack's number-driven quant perspective was able to adapt. But he explained it: "I think anyone in my position would feel urgency. That calls for strong measures." In effect, with his back against the wall of another potentially losing year, he had to go where he had not gone before. He had to think about people, and the relationships among them at different levels. He had to act like a leader, and assume responsibility for changing his organization's culture. He had to figure out how.

By the end of 2022, as we were racing past the pandemic, Comet was turning a profit. "But you know," he said, "there's a new sense of commitment among my staff. Okay, we're doing better because the market is better – but everyone is also pulling harder." What he did not mention is that he had produced this change. He had recognized that quant-thinking was insufficient at this juncture in the life of his business, and he would have to involve himself with how people related to the business. He appears to have done so with grace.

As a final measure, Jack decided to mentor a few of the younger partners, and explain how he had engineered the turn-around. "Obviously," he said, "I won't be around forever, and the firm will eventually need new blood. It's the nature of comets to disappear for a while and then, predictably, to return – I want these people to be ready. He organized monthly seminars on management. Some months, he focused on competition (as he put it, "out-thinking the other guys"). But he also stressed that management meant keeping your eyes focused on the client. "I want people to feel comfortable relating to clients," he told me. "That's how I really did it." Jack told me that these mentorship sessions were becoming famous. "Some business school guy came around and asked to attend a few. Given my background, I had to laugh."

But mentorship is serious. Jack took it seriously. "It's another part of taking on responsibility," he told me. I wondered if he'd someday write a textbook on how to lead in a turn-around situation. Big-name guys like Lee Iacocca had done it. Why couldn't an everyday leader like Jack?

In the meantime, and along the way, he has learned that:

- Leaders take responsibility for the culture of their business, and do what is necessary to change it.

- The culture of a business depends on whether people feel part of that culture – it's a leader's responsibility to ensure that they do.
- Taking responsibility often means getting out side of your comfort zone, and breaking old habits of thinking.
- You can make changes, but the people around you must understand why you are making them.
- If you want to change a business that you lead, you often have to change yourself to become the leader that it needs.
- Difficult times sometimes demand entirely new approaches.
- Mentorship is integral to leadership responsibilities.

It took Jack a while to figure all this out. But he took it on board. Ultimately, he ran with it. The Street has begun to notice (and copy) the changes. "That's confirmation," Jack told me, "apart from the improved bottom line."

This story concerns an investment banker who assumes moral responsibility for his firm when it faces an ethical dilemma. He could just coast along and follow the crowd. But he steps up, takes the ethical high ground, and persuades everyone else that he's right. This is ethical leadership.

So, as you read this story, ask yourself:

- *Would I risk of confronting people whose ethical positions are questionable, and likely to damage the group that I lead?*
- *Do I put my own comfort ahead of the group's welfare?*
- *Do define responsibility as including an ethical component, especially when the effect of taking the ethical position may not emerge until well past the time that I take my stand?*
- *Am I good at persuading others – who may be resistant – that the ethical position is finally the least risky?*

The young man in this story learns to navigate these questions. He brings the higher-ups around to his position. Ask yourself if you have the stamina and skill to do the same.

Leaders Take Moral Responsibility

Your Conscience Is the Ultimate Guide

I have never bought the Brooklyn Bridge, even by mistake. But I know who could sell it to anyone. After five minutes with Bruce, I saw myself as the owner of a phantom piece of New York infrastructure. Bruce had the salesman's knack – he made you feel special, discerning, ready to make your next prescient move.

How? He complimented my beard (it was Freud-length, a feature of my psychiatric practice), and my tie (he said that my beard "set it off"). He noticed the

Chinese calligraphy on the wall, and how my Persian rug was reflected in the glass of its frame. I was intrigued. "You didn't intend that effect," he told me, "but I'm sure it results from a deep-down aesthetic." I sat back and waited for the pitch.

As it turned out, Bruce *was* a salesman, but not of anything so tangible as a brick and steel landmark. He was an investment banker, who presented "deals" to customers anxious to speculate. They stood to earn millions if the deals worked out in line with projections. "I just got an investor for an EV venture in Mexico," he told me. "Mexico turns out lithium-ion batteries faster than we do, and this venture has real potential." (I resisted the urge to buy shares myself – besides, the deal was sketchy and I can't use info from clients that way.) So, I wondered what Bruce's issue was. Why was he in my office? Surely, no one was suffering from buyer's remorse – he lived in a world of *caveat emptor*, which everyone accepted.

I waited. He explained.

"I've just been appointed interim director of the firm's Southern Hemisphere Group," he said, "and I'd love to get the permanent position. But I have an ethical problem – it might stand in the way." In other words, Bruce was expected to execute deals that the firm devised, while from a personal perspective, he might selectively want to decline. I had seen these leadership challenges before, and they are never easy to sort out.

The questions they raise are complex. Is a leader primarily loyal to the organization, making sure it makes the most money (or the most of anything it's supposed to produce)? Or should every person (no matter their position) be primarily loyal to themselves, and adhere to their own ethical standards? How do we balance the two, especially since the underlying issues are rarely black-and-white?

I asked Bruce if he could square the interests of the firm with his own. That is, could he somehow compromise? If he could, then he could finesse the dilemma.

But he came at my question from the opposite perspective.

"Yeah," he said, "the *firm* would have to compromise – it's better off if it doesn't pursue the deal. But it's not my call, and my boss wants me to proceed. He's not exactly testing me, but I think I'll be passed over if I seem refractory."

In effect, Bruce thought he was expected to lead, but not lead so much that he ruffled the higher-ups' feathers. Was he supposed to be a go-along-get-along leader, who occupied the role but didn't define it? That seemed to be what troubled him. He didn't want a bare title. He *did* want the position if he could make it his own. "I need to feel comfortable doing what I do," he said. "I'm not even sure it's legitimate to occupy a position if you know it will put you in a tight ethical spot."

Bruce was a thoughtful guy. So, I wondered, was his boss bothered by similar questions, or had he compromised his standards to get where he was? In practical terms, was he likely to cut Bruce some slack, just because he realized how deals can sometimes seem "off"? Or was Bruce right in assuming that failing to march to the designated drummer would effectively end his chances of retaining the directorship? I hoped it would not come down to a contest of wills, and that Bruce and his boss might still reason together.

But before I could assess Bruce's position relative to his boss, I asked whether his boss had considered the deal's questionable aspects. "He knows about them," Bruce said. "The lawyers have laid them all out, but they're hazy, and you can see what you want to see." Apparently, the boss chose to see Yes. It was Bruce's view vs. that of a guy with much more experience (who also held sway over Bruce's pending appointment).

"My problem," Bruce said, "is that I don't care if my boss has more institutional standing. I just can't buy how he sees this deal, and I think it will hurt the firm if we accept it." What I heard, was that Bruce – even as interim director – felt responsible for leading the firm in an ethically/legally sound direction (he saw ethics and the law as convergent, a suspect position among most investment bankers). From an institutional perspective, his views did not count as much as his boss'. "I've only been at the firm five years," he said, "and before that I was in grad school. To my boss, it's like 'Why should we listen to him?'"

Bruce was in a difficult position. He had not yet paid his dues in terms of years, while he awkwardly opposed the views of someone who had.

Still, I didn't want to advise Bruce one way or another until I knew more about the deal itself. "Tell me why you have qualms," I said.

I got a lesson in international economics.

The deal would develop a 12,000-acre palm oil plantation in the Amazon rain forest. Palm oil? It's huge. More than half of all packaged products Americans consume contain palm oil – lipstick, soaps, detergents, even ice cream. The oil palm is attractive because it offers a far greater yield at a lower production cost than other oil-producing plants (say, safflower). Global demand is increasing, and plantations are spreading across Asia, Africa, and Latin America. But Bruce told me, "Plantations are displacing tropical forests – the critical habitats for endangered species and lifelines for indigenous communities." I got the ethical point.

But was the project legally dubious?

Bruce said it was, because burning of forests to clear the land created greenhouse gases. "The Paris Agreement set goals to combat climate change," he told me, "and both the U.S. and Brazil signed on. So how – at least within the agreement's spirit – can we offer this deal?" Now I understood. I recalled stories of smoke and haze in Asia, where forests were cleared for development. "Then there's the question of soil erosion and the pollution of groundwater," he said. "Palm oil mills create tons of effluent – and even if the authorities look the other way, it's still borderline if there are no counter-measures."

The problem was with local enforcement, he said. "We're getting into technicalities," he said. "But the agreement is still the agreement, and Brazil still has laws about soil and water." This local apathy (read: notorious corruption) was the so-called grey area. I asked what could be done.

Bruce said, for example, that if the acreage could be relocated – perhaps to an area already been cleared, but then abandoned – then he could support the deal. "I suggested that to my boss," he told me, "but it was a non-starter. There would be a delay, and a lot of renegotiation, and the firm wanted to move while the market was hot."

So, I asked where things stood. Bruce sighed, "When I told my boss I couldn't take the lead – that there would be blowback and my reputation would suffer – he said that was silly. 'You're the right guy for this,' he said, 'and when you pull it off, you'll be in position to get the Director's job.'" Bruce had tried to sound practical (invoking his "reputation"), but his boss breezed right past him, appealing instead to ambition. "He even said he'd discussed the deal at the C-Suite level of *his* boss, and there was solid commitment to moving ahead."

The deck appeared to be stacked against him. So, now what?

Bruce was a team player, and wanted to promote his firm's business. He also wanted the experience of taking the lead on an important deal. "But," he said, "it's *because* I care about the company that I have to voice my objections – and then follow through if I think I'm right. I can't just wash my hands and then 'lead' by following everyone else." He saw the paradox in what his boss was asking of him.

More to the point, Bruce articulated a complex, multi-dimensional sense of responsibility, encompassing the firm as well as himself. "My ethical sense," he said, "covers how I operate as a company-man *and* as a human being concerned about the law and the climate. They're not in conflict – though the higher-ups think they are." Bruce was acting like a leader, responsible for his company's ethical standing which, he hoped, would reflect his own view of what a responsible person would do. "It's the only thing I can do," he said.

Bruce knew that he could go behind his boss' back, and alert other people on his team to an ethical/legal quandary that should be avoided. But he thought he'd only get in trouble if someone went behind *his* back, and alerted his boss. "I'm going straight to the C-Suite," he told me. "If they want to fire me, I'll risk it – but at least I won't keep driving myself crazy with this." It's a fact that when we repress our sense of responsibility, and just let things slide, we never shake the feeling that we could have done more. At inflection points, the feeling flares up, and we regret our previous inaction.

A couple of weeks went by before I saw Bruce again. Obviously, he had not yet mustered enough courage to visit the C-Suite. "I'm pondering how to present all this," he said, "since I don't want to seem moralistic. But I do think that lawyers – being lawyers – cite risks, then leave the decision up to the client." What he meant, was that they didn't want to bear responsibility for the "decision." He didn't have much time, however, since his boss was pressing him to start.

Another couple of weeks went by. Bruce had finally talked to the C-Suite guy with oversight of his boss. "He decided to pull back. The reason he gave was something about insurance – but I knew I had touched a nerve." The guy did not fire him.

"What did you say that turned him around," I asked. Bruce was a terrific salesman. "I told him," he said, "that *he* bore ultimate responsibility for the firm. 'Okay, I'm afraid of any blowback towards me, but what about blowback from the press, or activists, or even some of the firm's partners – it's your responsibility to make sure that doesn't happen.'" This was clever. Let the guy know he was in this as deep as anyone who promoted it, and that nothing about it was pretty. "You clearly got the guy's attention," I said. "Once someone hears 'responsibility,' they start to consider consequences – for themselves and for everyone."

The C-Suite guy did consider them, it seems. "He must have spoken to my boss too," Bruce said. "I wonder if he made the same argument." We will never know.

In any case, his boss seemed disgruntled for several weeks. He never mentioned the deal again, which he had obviously thought would benefit him too. But eventually, another deal emerged – this time, a zinc mine in Peru – and Bruce got picked to head it. "I think I'm back on track he said."

In fact, he was. When we last spoke, he had received the permanent position. At the formal announcement, which the C-Suite guy attended, Bruce was cited for "keeping track of the firm's best interests" – an anodyne reference to internal warfare over a bunch of palm trees. But to Bruce, it was vindication, an affirmation of his ethical judgment. "Sometimes," he told me, "grey gets darker the closer you look."

Bruce learned a lot during the experience, for example:

- In taking responsibility, a leader cannot just follow the path of least resistance – that's an abdication of responsibility.
- Ethical leadership may entail personal risks – you should be prepared to assume them.
- Leaders do not just look to serve or vindicate themselves – they seek to promote the interests of their organizations.
- When someone else says that an issue is hazy and ethically uncertain, that provides no cover for you – you need to think on your own, and go to bat for your views.

None of this came easily to Bruce. But he finally realized that unless he acted in accordance with his own best assessment of the situation, he would look back on his failure – and wince – when he faced the next inflection point. So, he took a chance. It worked out for the best. It might not have, but he told me, "My conscience is clear." Taking responsibility has that effect.

This story concerns a leader in the art world who assumes the responsibility of finding her successor. How does she find the right person? How does she groom her successor to ensure a successful transition? Neither of these questions have easy answers, but she succeeds.

So, as you read this story, ask yourself these questions:

- *Am I psychologically prepared to face the need for a succession plan?*
- *Am I equipped to negotiate with a chosen successor, so that the transition occurs smoothly?*
- *Will I allow time for my successor to accommodate to his or her new position?*
- *Will I allow stakeholders in the transition, especially an organization's employees, to participate in managing the transition?*
- *Am I an effective mentor, helping my successor without insisting that they become my clone?*
- *Am I open to new ideas, so that the succession serves to extend the capabilities of my organization?*

Of course, "succession" requires a leader to eventually stand back. But they can still help to make the succession a creative process. They can still mentor their successor even as that person brings new ideas. The people in this story work hard at succession – it cannot succeed any other way.

Leaders Are Responsible for Making Succession Plans

Taking Responsibility for Succession Means Being Responsible for One's Successor

When Lisa practiced law, maybe 20 years ago, she never occupied a corner office. But everyone envied her. Her practice was "interesting." Unlike the other partners, whose clients were corporations, Lisa worked with artists, galleries, collectors, and museums. She got invited to openings and auctions, and accepted first editions of numbered lithographs as part of her fee. She was a regular at international art fairs. "It was a charmed life," she told me. "I could have made a go of it."

But Lisa was being modest. By the time she had left the practice, she was known throughout New York (which, in art circles, equates to the world), as a top practitioner of Art Law. It's a small, rarefied field but, in places like New York and London, it matters.

As a body of law, Art Law draws on an array of disciplines – copyright, contract, tort, tax, commercial, Constitutional, and international law – to facilitate and regulate the creation, sale, collection, and display of fine and visual art. It also deals with valuation and appraisal, as in the sale of "multiples" (identical copies made specifically for sale). As art crosses borders, art lawyers disentangle customs regulations. When an heiress donates art to a museum, art lawyers help structure the deal to avoid crushing estate taxes.

But beneath that commercial-sounding veneer, art lawyers are political actors, mediating claims of cultural appropriation on behalf of indigenous populations.

They stand in for diplomats when countries demand the return of artistic patrimony. So, of course, they are into archaeology. They advise the police and the FBI when art goes missing. They get involved in fraud cases, counterfeiting investigations, and the law of war. They advise TV producers on the machinery of art world thrillers. "I got some script credits," Lisa said, "and once I played a cameo of myself."

Yet when Lisa came to see me a while back, she wanted out. I confess that before I asked why, I fantasized about that old Eddie Murphy movie, *Trading Places*, where I could fall into her gig and she could take up mine. But, instead, I just said "Tell me more." I guess I knew what she would say before she said it.

"I've had enough with billable hours," she told me. "I just think there's more to life." It emerged that she was seeking to connect more directly to art. She was taking studio classes at the Art Institute. "It's changing the way I think," she said. "I'm becoming a visual person." I heard the old Foucauldian claim that vision supersedes language as our primary mode of apprehension. In effect, Lisa was making that transition, leaving a profession founded on words for one where they eye comes first. But how would this play out?

I asked what she next had in mind. "It sounds like you want to stay involved with art, just in a different capacity," I said. "You're not thinking of *making* it, I assume." She wasn't, so we talked about how she could remain in the art world – just not as an art lawyer.

"I have an idea," Lisa told me. During her classes at the Institute, she had made friends with people whom she called "real artists." They made art for a living, and were trying to perfect their technique. They were also, apparently, trying to survive in a profession where some artists make millions and everyone else subsists. "Maybe I can help them," she said. "Not as a lawyer, but as someone who looks out for them." As she defined it, their real problem was that they didn't understand the market. For most of them, there was almost no market at all – if they sold a painting or a lithograph, it was usually without an agent or a gallery behind them. "They don't have any way of establishing their own worth," she told me. "They need a paywall."

As we continued to talk, I began to see the shape of her idea. She would be a different kind of artist's rep. "I won't exactly sell images," she said, "but access to images." A generation ago, this was a new concept, made possible by digitization . . . of everything.

She would set up a site to license the use of artwork for specific purposes – brochures, posters, book covers, postcards at the Met – for an appropriate fee. As proprietor of the site, which she called ArtAccess, she would take a portion of the fee (much as galleries did, except this would be a digital gallery). "In a way," she said, "it will be like creating multiples of every image – if the cost is lower, the volume will more than make up for it." I could see where she was going. But, of course, the trick would be to sign up enough artists to make the site a profitable venture.

Lisa had an idea for that as well. She started with a few big names, on the assumption that other artists would then take notice. The estates of Chagall and Miro became her first participants. Then she came to the estate of Paul Klee. "I had to convince them," she said, "that licensing the art wasn't cheapening it – they could specify whatever conditions they wanted, and could require proper acknowledgment." Finally, her friends from the Institute caught the bug. "Maybe I'll sell a few pictures to a collector," one told her, "but this is how to get known more broadly. I could get discovered." For Lisa, the site represented a community, where people and artists literally mingled online.

She was so inspired, in fact, that she started a nonprofit organization dedicated to advocating for artists' rights. It was called WorldArt, and it monitored copyright legislation and legal developments everywhere, making the point that artists could only make a living if their rights were adequately protected. "I have reps in the EU, the Asia Pacific region, and in South America. If an artist feels they are getting ripped off, we know whom to talk to." The organization became so vocal – and effective – that it was written up in major art journals. It was cited in the *Congressional Record* and in amicus briefs filed with the Supreme Court. If anything, Lisa had become even more well-known in art circles than she had been as a lawyer.

More to the point, she was now a leader in an important space. "I'm making the world safe for artists," she joked, though I knew she was utterly serious. I also assumed that having reached this position, she had achieved her goal of moving past her legal practice. For a while, I even seemed to be right.

But after a few years, Lisa was back. "I've had quite a trajectory," she told me, "but the best trajectories end in a legacy. I want to think about mine." In a way, I thought she was channeling all the Miros and Klees – and their peers – on her site, whose legacies were enormous. So, I said, "just think about how you've raised people's consciousness about compensating artists – that's a legacy." But she had in mind something more concrete.

Some years ago, Bill Gates had approached her, offering to buy her business and the underlying digital rights. "He even offered to fund WorldArt for the next 25 years if we could make a deal," she said. But they couldn't make a deal. "I guess it all seemed too impersonal, like what I would have done back at the law firm. I wanted people at the helm that I knew, whom I could trust to carry on the way I would."

So, we discussed how she could transition out of the business – while still preserving its character. "You've put together a good team," I said, "and maybe one of them could serve as president." She nodded, but observed that there was still the underlying question of ownership. "I can't take it public," she said. "It's a family business, and that's the only way it will keep to its principles." Okay, then who was family?

Lisa had raised the classic issue of intra-family succession, with all the challenges that *Succession* had dramatized over several agonizing seasons. Leaders cannot lead forever. They must manage a succession effectively, or risk the demise, disruption, or distortion of the business. Lisa knew this. She just wasn't sure how to bring it off.

I asked whether she had any children who might want to own the company.

Well, there was a daughter, Pearl, who was involved in the next generation of the art market. Taking a cue from her mother – but, she insisted, leaving her behind – Pearl had started a company that represented artists and their NFTs (non-fungible tokens, which give digital images a unique code, permitting them to be owned by a particular person). This was a new, hot area. Even Melania Trump had ventured to sell an NFT of her wide-brimmed hat. The ethos of the whole regime was at least questionable but, Lisa told me, "Pearl thinks I'm old-school." She thought they could never work together effectively. "We see the art world differently."

Still, I thought it was worth a shot. Pearl understood and loved her mother, and understood and loved the art market. Wasn't some form of synergy possible, provided there was sufficient imagination (and flexibility) on all sides? I suggested that the three of us meet to find a way forward. "Part of being a leader," I said, "is bringing people together around a successful succession. Now that's your responsibility." In effect, I was asking Lisa to participate in a succession effort, including all the give-and-take it would require before everyone could agree.

So, Lisa, Pearl, and I started talking. Pearl acknowledged that while she joked about ArtAccess ("What am I going to tell my friends?"), it was still a money-maker. As a businesswoman, she saw its potential. "I think," she said, "it has room for improvement."

We were getting somewhere.

But, surprisingly, the first sticking point came from Lisa. While she now felt responsible for planning the succession, she felt hampered by a responsibility for the current employees. Privately, she asked me, "How can I just tell them 'Okay, here's the new owner?' They might resent her just being 'anointed,' and coming in without learning the business from the ground up." I agreed that her concern was legitimate. Sometimes, a leader's responsibilities may (or may seem to) conflict. But in this instance, there was an obvious workaround. "Just kind of ease her in, and let the employees help train her," I proposed. That is, when people feel part of a transition, they won't see their interests as bound to conflict with it. "You're not co-opting them," I said, "just letting them own the transition insofar as it affects them."

This whole experience was as new to Lisa as it would be to everyone else, and it mattered that she – as well as everyone – feel comfortable in managing it.

So, in that spirit, Lisa, Pearl, and I kept talking – this time, focused on how to ensure the employees' participation. We decided that during a period of about three or four years, Pearl would occupy a mid-level position, learning the business and everyone's role in it (there were 25 employees and some interns).

During this period, she would still run her own business – or, at least, supervise the Gen Xers who worked there virtually, and were mainly ensuring that the auctions ran smoothly). Once she began to get the hang of things, the transition could itself transition into possibly merging the two operations into a more comprehensive suite of services, better representing artists and their work. Of course, there might be incompatibilities between the companies' cultures, but she would be better able to assess that as she got to know her new colleagues. "That's something my mother and I can work on," she told me, making room for her mother now and down the road. Her openness to Lisa's perspective was reassuring.

At this point, about two years in, Pearl is easing her way towards the top position. Lisa is still the titular owner, and will not formally make the hand-over until Pearl (and everyone) feels ready. "Right now, I'm more an *eminence grise,*" she told me. "It's hard to just let go, and maybe I'll assume a new role as Chairman." But Lisa recognizes her responsibility to allow Pearl to finally take charge. "It's like my actual role is that of mentor-in-chief. The employees are helping, but I have a feeling for the company, and that's what I want to leave her with." I think that's right. In grooming the next leader, the current one should give him or her a sense of the company's place in its ecosystem – in this case, a tough art market, where artists need the means to get a fair shake. As evidence that Lisa's mentoring is having that effect, Pearl also agreed to manage WorldArt. "The business and the nonprofit are about the same thing," she told me when we last met.

But apart from what Pearl is learning, I'm struck by how Lisa's mentorship is working both ways. That is, Lisa is learning from Pearl. "She has a more happening style," Lisa told me. "She operates more on instinct than I do, and when you're dealing with people who revel in the sensory, that's probably right." I heard Foucault again, but so what? If both parties share common principles, then there will be a better, less drama-prone transition. Mother-daughter relationships can be fraught (this one certainly had its challenges), so the more that each of them can think in sync, the easier the succession will be.

So, during this process, Lisa acquired some real skills about managing the succession, including:

- Leaders are responsible for designing a succession plan, and then for helping to ensure its success.
- Intra-family succession may entail the added challenge of differing, generational perspectives – but these can be negotiated provided there is goodwill.
- Mentorship plays a crucial role in any succession plan – it's a leader's responsibility (to her organization and to the person next in line) to be an attentive, effective mentor.
- Mentorship can work in both directions – be open to new ideas.
- Succession plans do not affect just the current and future leadership – they also affect other stake-holders, e.g., employees.

- Leaders allow those with an interest in the transition to participate in how it is managed.
- Ceding leadership to a new generation is always hard, but it is inevitable – so manage it as gracefully as possible.
- Where a leader perceives a conflict between managing a succession and fulfilling her other responsibilities, it is important to find a workaround.

So far, Lisa and Pearl are managing well. Their responsibilities are shifting, as Pearl takes on more and Lisa stands back. That is the nature of succession. But, as Lisa told me, "I want to put 'success' into this succession." It seems to be there already.

***

The stories in this chapter are not just about "taking charge." Responsibility is so much more than acting the part of a drill sergeant. Rather, it concerns how you address complex challenges, and ensure that they do not overwhelm you and your organization. It's about acting from the perspective of tomorrow and the next day – that is, not just accepting the status quo. The responsible leader is a change agent, ensuring that the people they work can perform optimally (where the leader sets the example).

Ethics matter in leadership, if only because people are always watching – somebody somewhere sometime will finally have the goods. So, it's important to ensure that your organization is on an ethically sound footing. It's easier to avoid mistakes than to clean up after them. It may *seem* easier to act as though nothing is wrong . . . but that's shortsighted. It never works in the long run. Own your mistakes, acknowledge the challenges and headwinds, and take defensive actions to keep things from deteriorating (and, ideally, to fix them).

While leaders are, necessarily, outward-facing – and concerned with how their organization acts in the world – they must also be introspective. In these stories, each leader (in his or her own way) contends with personal attitudes, habits, memories, regrets. They need to reconcile their feelings with their leadership aspirations. In some cases, the undertaking is dramatic, resulting in a major personal turn-around. It is always hard work. Leaders must perform the personal work that precedes – that is prerequisite – to their public work as a leader. This work, which begins with the most personal, ramifies outward into the organizations they lead and, finally, into that organization's effectiveness in the world at large. So, leaders must examine who they are; who they want to be; and how best to evolve.

The stories in this chapter demonstrate that:

- Leaders who accept responsibility must usually define that responsibility – they should not shrink from the risk.

- Risk is inherent in leadership – the responsible leader learns how to manage it to mitigate its impact on the organization that he or she leads.
- Part of responsibility is seeing a challenge in one's own life, or in society, and scaling up the potential remedy to mitigate that challenge on a large scale.
- Stasis is the opposite of assuming responsibility – leaders produce positive change, they get out of their comfort zones, they shift the prevailing paradigm towards the greater good.
- Responsibility comes in many forms, not least in arranging for who will replace you – the transition to new leadership is inevitable, so manage it gracefully.

I know the people in these stories. We have kept up. It is a curious fact that once they became leaders, and learned how to take responsibility, they continued finding new ways to exercise it effectively. Responsibility can be exhilarating. It allows you to watch the effect of your work in real time, and to contemplate it going forward. The work is hard, but it's good work. I am reminded of Howard Garder's great book, *Good Work: When Excellence and Ethics Meet*. The best leaders could take that title as a motto.

References

Armstrong, Jesse (creator). *Succession* (2018–2023).
Gardner, Howard et al. *Good Work: When Ethics and Excellence Meet* (New York: Basic Books), 2001.
Iacocca, Lee. *An Autobiography* (New York: Bantam Books), 1994.
Landis, John (director). *Trading Places* (1983).

Conclusion

Everyday Leadership draws on my experience advising clients who, for an array of reasons, were called on to take a leadership position. Likewise, everyday leadership is based on experience – we learn to lead as challenges arise, and we develop skills to address them. Thus, *in the process of leading*, we learn to communicate, to compromise, and to collaborate so that others can help further our objectives. Basically, we experience our way to becoming a leader. In this sense, we don't need what might be called the "leadership gene," that rare combination of family background, elite schooling, and early involvement in an environment where the exercise of power is second nature (think of the Kennedys, the Roosevelts, or Winston Churchill). Everyday leaders pick up the skills they need, often through trial and error, and through a willingness to change course (and sometimes, features of their personality) as circumstances change. They *focus* on being a leader, and integrate what they learn into their own, evolving path through the world.

To experience leadership as a type of constant learning and assimilation is the opposite of linearity. Just like any other type of ongoing experience, this type is full of zigs and zags. The aspiring leader – and even one of long standing – must be open to it. As this book demonstrates, so much of successful leadership depends on how we think about leadership, that is, on how we approach and continually redefine our tasks, our objectives, and even ourselves. Thus, while leadership is not necessarily an "adventure" (with all the thrills that adventurists seek), it still may be full of surprise, tough going, and some hair-raising near-misses. That's okay. The best leaders find a way to fight uphill battles and rearguard actions (even simultaneously!) because they must. Of course, they may panic and break a sweat. But they keep going, assimilating experience, refining their goals and their strategies.

I wrote *Everyday Leadership* to offer readers a type of vicarious experience, where they see how others (like themselves) grappled with the challenges of leadership. Think of it as an experience accelerator. The case studies allow readers to participate in the strategies – the thought processes – of these leaders, and compare those strategies to how they themselves might have approached

DOI: 10.4324/9781003437635-7

a similar situation. While everyone is different, we naturally learn from the experience of people we can relate to (that is, we learn more from someone who starts a local music club than from a Kennedy). My hope is that, after a while, readers will not just participate in how these people navigate a challenge, but *anticipate* how such a challenge should be navigated. At that point, readers may begin to sense what everyday leadership feels like. They may begin to feel more confident – readier to take on a challenge should the need arise.

In this regard, *Everyday Leadership* encourages everyday leaders not to stand back in awe of a challenge but, rather, to take its measure appropriately. Reluctance, and sometimes even fear, can be debilitating, while self-confidence (you know your stuff!) can energize you. So much depends on how you assess yourself in relation to a challenge. Right-sizing a challenge (I can learn a new technology, a new set of rules) will help overcome the sense that a challenge is beyond you. In Irving Feldman's *All of Us Here*, an apt passage suggests that we are just as large as our burdens allow, and no smaller than the task at hand requires. In other words, we're up-to-it, provided our perspective (on ourselves) is adjusted accordingly.

As you have now realized, this book examines what leaders see when they look inside themselves – what still needs improvement, how to compensate for mistakes, whether to share more responsibility. This is because a) I am a psychiatrist, so I study how self-estimation affects how one acts, and b) effective leaders project self-assurance, and a firm sense of understanding a challenge. They want to get to a place where they are credible as leaders. An uncertain leader who displays uncertainty rarely inspires confidence in his or her leadership. So, my objective throughout has been to help you find the self-confidence – to help you develop the skills – to believe in yourself as a leader.

Everyday Leadership examines five, inter-related qualities required for leadership:

Vision – You don't have to be a visionary like Bill Gates, whose famous book, *The Road Ahead*, forecast how tech (which he helped pioneer) would transform how we live and work. But you do need a reasonably coherent goal and, more to the point, a sense of purpose (for example, like Larry in this book, who set out to expand the scope of medical literature). You need to recognize that any vision – though it guides your objectives – is malleable. That is, it can change, and you should accept the change. My client Larry did not end up where he expected to because, in response to chance encounters, what he *thought* he wanted became something different. He was surprised, but he changed personally along with his vision. We need to work with (reassessing, redefining) any vision we develop, making the most of it based on our circumstances.

For the cover of *Everyday Leadership*, I chose an image of a compass. Before GPS became standard equipment, compasses indicated "true north," so that we could determine the direction to follow. We could calculate any redirection based on the deviation from true north. My sense of a leader's vision is very much like how sailors, pioneers, and everyday travelers used to determine the best way forward. They knew where they wanted to go, and understood they might have to alter direction if a storm – or other challenge – arose. Unlike GPS, compasses can't provide advance notice of some looming challenge. They demand a kind of canny independence based on the art of the journeyer, who switches gears and adjusts the course as some obstacle comes into view. (If you've seen *Titanic*, you know just what I mean.) This need for quick, nimble response distinguishes the best leaders.

Determination and Flexibility – Flexibility is a necessary component of determination, since stubborn leaders (who may even take pride in their rigidity and unwillingness to bend) are never successful. Unbending leaders may think they seem strong but, in fact, they just seem unimaginative, unable to seize opportunities that present themselves but then may disappear. What's required, therefore, is a 360° vision, so that you can adapt to circumstances as they develop. You need a type of strategic imagination, where you adhere to your sense of purpose but redefine how you pursue it. Nobody just thinks "Oh, an obstacle is just another opportunity." Leadership, like life, is more complicated. But the best leaders learn to think around obstacles, which may entail a sometime radical change in plans. Think of my client Denise, who discovers that compromise (with other people, with her sense of herself) is crucial if she is to achieve a leadership position.

Planning and Organization – If you can't devise a plan, and then organize your way towards achieving it, you will never be a competent leader. Lots of people can concoct a vision ("I wanna lead a mission to Mars!"), but unless they can follow through with the day-to-day nitty-gritty, they do not stand a chance. Planning and organization require attention to detail, and a type of consummate involvement that keeps track of problems before they develop into major headaches. It requires seeing (or, at least, thinking) around corners. It requires playing the long game. It also requires letting go, and an ability to delegate. The best leaders form great teams. They spot situations that need attention, and find people who can address them. So, from an attitudinal perspective, planning and organization require that you recognize talents in other people and deploy such people effectively. Thus, while planning and organization may seem like you're just moving boxes around on an organization chart, it actually requires an ability to animate those boxes – you're finding, encouraging, and inspiring loyalty in people who you hope will support your objectives. Like all the other characteristics of leadership, planning and organization come down to establishing and maintaining relationships.

Communication and Collaboration – Humans communicate. At the most obvious level, we employ language to convey ideas. More subtly, we signal each other through how we behave – for example, how receptive we are to others' ideas, and whether we'll commit to objectives that benefit people other than ourselves. Remember, in an organization (especially a small one) everyone sees everything. They pick up on our actions, and interpret them through the prism of their own best interests. So, as leaders, we need to ensure that our actions are not interpreted in ways that undermine own interests. Communication becomes an exercise in vigilance. We should prevent people around us from drawing the wrong conclusions. What we do, buttressed by what we say, must project honesty, and a concern for those who it's our responsibility to lead. We cannot come off as self-involved. Thus, whether or not people are organized into formal teams, they should feel part of a conjectural team where everyone counts. You inspire confidence in your leadership when you help people feel this type of involvement.

Of course, in organizations we work *with* other people, either in formal or informal collaborations, over short or extended periods. In the chapter "Communication and Collaboration," I stressed that leaders learn how to leverage collaboration, so that their collaborators help further the leaders' objectives. Thus, collaboration is not just a natural consequence of working side-by-side with others. Rather, it is instrumental, a strategic vehicle for engaging the talents of other people and turning them towards our advantage. In this effort, we need to make these people feel like part of what we're working towards. They need to feel that the benefits of collaboration flow in both directions. So, effective communication is an element of effective collaboration. At bottom, leaders use communication to inspire loyalty, hard work, and strategic thinking in people with whom they work.

Responsibility – Leaders do not just take credit for things that go their way. They accept responsibility for mistakes, and set about trying to fix them. In this regard, they are more than merely honest – they're candid, and responsive to questions from people affected by their actions. Thus, they are aware of the stake-holders, both inside and external to their organization. They respond to their needs. They take responsibility for the whole organization, as well as its penumbra of customers, clients, and anyone with an interest in how the organization operates. They know that government at various levels may be interested, so they take responsibility for compliance with every rule that may come into play. The buck truly stops with them, and they accept that.

But the best leaders are also proactive. Think about my client Bruce, a mid-level leader who saved his company from promoting a risky venture. He didn't have to undertake this effort, which posed significant internal risks to himself. But he felt responsible, in the best sense, for ensuring that his company adhered to the highest ethical standards. Why? Because he had cultivated an ethical turn of mind in himself, and refused to leave it at the door when he came to work each day. His leadership was finally applauded but, more importantly, he was able to live with himself. Taking responsibility – that is, stepping up to do what's right – is as much about one's own equanimity as it is making some pubic gesture. Leaders need to feel like they are their best selves.

Finally, I want to cite an aspect of responsibility that does not immediately come to mind when we discuss ethical standards or acknowledging (and fixing) mistakes. I'm referring to mentoring, which appears in two stories under "Responsibility." Mentoring involves cultivating the next generation of leaders to promote a smooth transition. It involves teaching and setting a good example. The person who you mentor should feel free to ask questions. Concomitantly, as a leader, you should feel free to judge, so long as your judgments are constructive and don't sound pejorative. In mentoring situations, the leader's responsibility is *both* to an organization (or profession at large) and to an individual. It is also to him- or herself, since leaders are unlikely to feel they have fulfilled their responsibility unless they have successfully mentored the next generation.

In this context, I am thinking of one of my own mentors, James Strain, M.D. Dr. Strain was a leader in the field of psychiatry, whose remarkable contributions included a method for contemporaneous record-keeping with a pen-entry system (more than a decade before the iPad) which supported more spontaneous interactions with patients. Yet while his work was celebrated, he was proudest of the generation of colleagues he had mentored (which ultimately included departments chairs, clinicians, and leaders in public policy). He saw this as his legacy. Looking back now, I would agree.

Of course, mentors ultimately need to let go of the reins. I recall one young doctor who I mentored who was more talented than I was – a gifted leader, once he learned the ropes. For a while, I was a bit envious. Why couldn't I imagine the projects that he could, and why couldn't I execute them so flawlessly? But then I realized that mentoring is about supporting the next generation – not envying them, much less holding them back when they might accomplish more than we can. So, as he glided towards the stratosphere, I gracefully let him go. My responsibility was to set him up . . . and I did that well.

So, what's the bottom line of *Everyday Leadership*? First, don't measure yourself against world-class leaders ("Well, I run a tight ship, but I'll never be [Bill Gates, Julia Child, Coco Chanel]"). Don't even imagine yourself in their situations. You're down on the ground in the real world, struggling with everyday problems that can still drive you nuts. You probably operate in obscurity. It's best, therefore, to have a workable vision that you pursue with energy and a willingness to change course as the need arises. It's best that you assume responsibility and take the high road since, in the end, you need to live with yourself. Everyday leadership is hard. But if you work at it, you'll be effective. You may even leverage your success into greater success. The point is to stay focused, think of the compass, and be ready to deal with what's next.

References

Cameron, James (director). *Titanic*, 1997.

Feldman, Irving. *All of Us Here* (New York: Viking), 1986.

Gates, Bill et al. *The Road Ahead* (New York: Viking), 1985.

Index

For Product Safety Concerns and Information please contact our EU representative GPSR@taylorandfrancis.com Taylor & Francis Verlag GmbH, Kaufingerstraße 24, 80331 München, Germany

Batch number: 09019479

Printed by Printforce, the Netherlands